Ready® Classroom
Mathematics

Grade K • Volume 1

Curriculum Associates®

NOT FOR RESALE

978-1-4957-8030-1
©2020–Curriculum Associates, LLC
North Billerica, MA 01862
No part of this book may be reproduced
by any means without written permission
from the publisher.
All Rights Reserved. Printed in USA.
6 7 8 9 10 11 12 13 14 15   21 20

BTS20r1

Contents

Contents (continued)

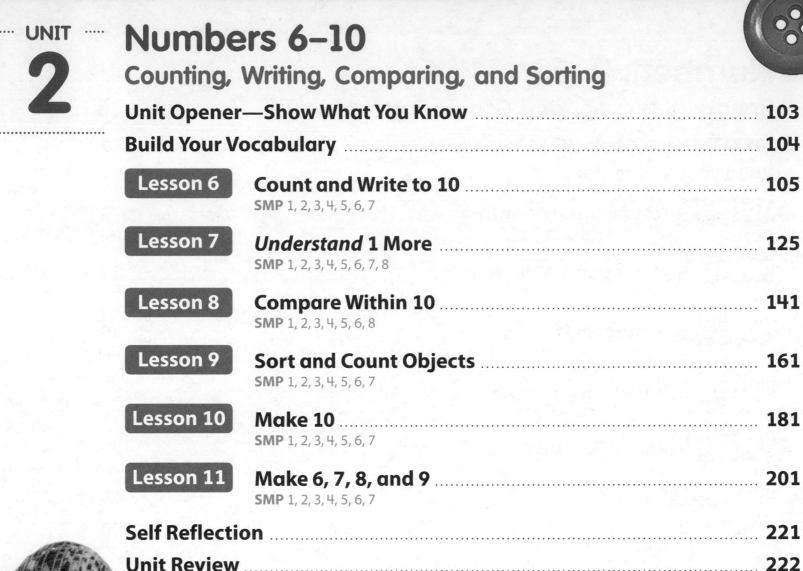

UNIT 3

Geometry
Naming, Comparing, and Building Shapes

Contents (continued)

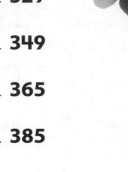

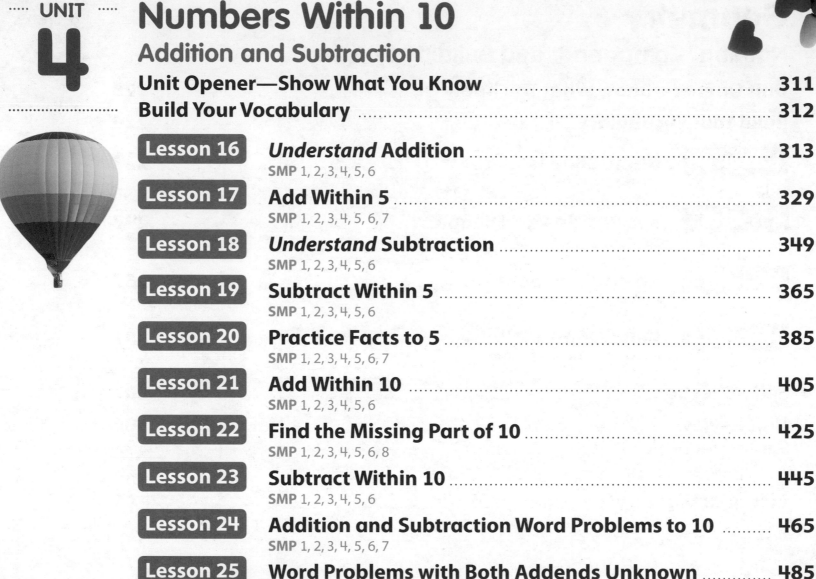

UNIT 5

Numbers 11–100
Teen Numbers and Counting by 1s and 10s

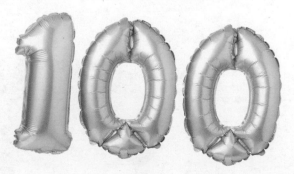

Contents (continued)

Show What You Know

Have children draw to show what they know about numbers 0–5. Tell children that after they have completed the unit, they will draw to show what they learned.

Build Your Vocabulary

My Math Words

Before the Unit

I can:

After the Unit

I can:

Have children draw to show what they know and what they have learned about numbers 0–5. Before starting the unit, have children draw to show what they know about numbers. After they have completed the unit, have them draw to show what they learned.

Understand Counting

Dear Family,

This week your child is exploring counting.

In class, your child will discuss reasons that people **count** and why counting is an important part of everyday life. For example, a teacher might count the books on a shelf to make sure there are enough for each child. Or a child might count the number of days until his or her birthday.

By counting objects in groups of 1 to 4, your child will also develop the understanding that when counting a group of objects, each **number** is associated with one object and the last number counted tells the total amount in the group. For example, when counting a group of 4 crayons, you might touch each crayon while saying a number: *1, 2, 3, 4. There are 4 crayons*. Or you might move each crayon to the side as it is counted.

1   2   3   4

There are 4 crayons.

Through learning what it means to count and developing strategies for keeping track of objects being counted, your child will start to build a strong foundation for success in math.

Invite your child to share what he or she knows about counting by doing the following activity together.

 **Counting**

Do this activity with your child to explore counting strategies.

Materials 3 cups, 9 pennies (or other small objects such as buttons or dried beans)

- Fill each of the cups with 2, 3, or 4 pennies (a different number in each cup).

- Have your child pour the pennies out of one cup and onto the table. Ask how many pennies are on the table.

- If your child has trouble counting the pennies, prompt him or her to use a strategy such as touching each penny as it is counted, moving each penny to the side as it is counted, or putting each penny in the cup as it is counted.

- Have your child put the pennies back in the cup and repeat with the other two cups. Then change the order of the three cups and do the activity again.

- If your child needs an extra challenge, here is a way to take the activity further. Have your child close his or her eyes and listen while you drop 1 to 4 pennies into a cup one at a time. Ask your child how many pennies are in the cup. Repeat several times.

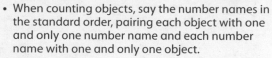

Learning Target

- When counting objects, say the number names in the standard order, pairing each object with one and only one number name and each number name with one and only one object.

SMP 1, 2, 3, 4, 5, 6

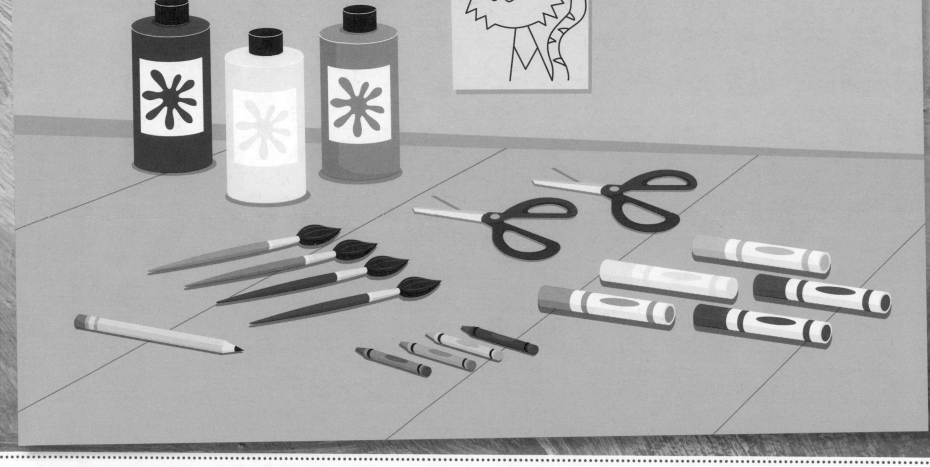

Have children name items to count in a picture and in the classroom. Ask: *What are some objects in the picture that you might count?* Have children name and circle some of the things they see that people might count.

Then lead the class on a walk around the classroom. Encourage children to think about what happens in each area and name items people might count.

Have children name items to count in a picture and think of other places people might count. Ask what someone might count at a sports field. Then discuss the soccer field scene and have children circle things people might count. Ask children to think about other places where people might count things and what they might count there. Help children to see people are counting in different places and at different times throughout the day.

Prepare for Counting

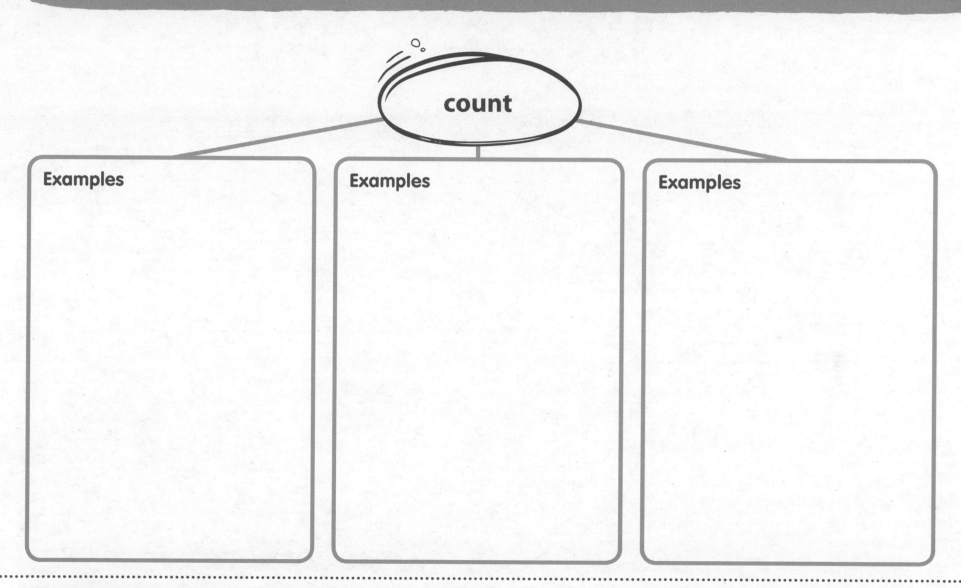

count

| Examples | Examples | Examples |

Have children show the meaning of the word *count*. Have children fill in each of the boxes to show the meaning of the word *count*. Tell children that they can use words, numbers, and pictures. Encourage them to show as many ideas as they can.

Have children name items to count in a picture and think of other places people might count. Ask what someone might count in nature. Then discuss the nature scene and have children circle things people might count.

Ask children to think about other places where people might count things and what they might count there. Ask children what they may have already counted today.

Develop Understanding of Counting

Why do we count?

Model It

Encourage children to discuss things people might count and why they want to count them. Then ask children to draw a picture of something they have counted or might want to count, such as stickers or other collectibles.

 Discuss It What are some other things that you count?

Connect It

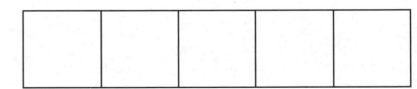

Have children count a set of objects. Have children color one square of the 5-frame for every object they count. Ask children to tell which number they counted to for each set of objects.

Discuss It How does coloring one square for each object help you count the group of objects?

Think About Counting

Why do we count?

Have children draw a picture of something they have counted or might like to count, such as stickers or blocks.

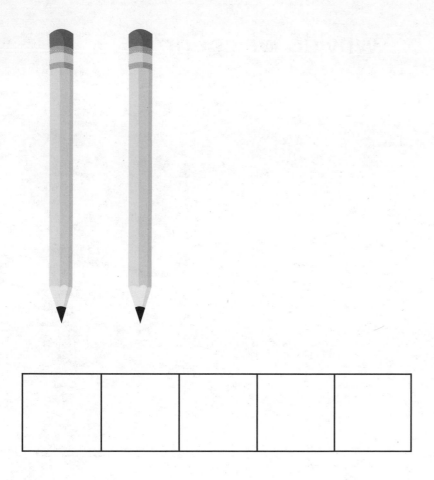

Have children count a set of objects. Have children color one square of the 5-frame for every object they count. Ask children to tell which number they counted to for each set of objects.

Develop Understanding of Counting

Model It

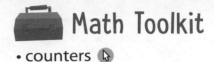 Math Toolkit
· counters

Have children match each counter to a tile to find the number of counters. Provide counters. Have children place them one at a time on the outline, then draw a line from the counter to a number, starting with 1. Have them circle the number that tells how many in all.

Discuss It How can you use the number tiles to help you find how many counters there are in all?

Connect It

| 1 | 2 | 3 | 4 |

| 1 | 2 | 3 | 4 |

Have children match each object to a tile to find the number of objects. Have children draw a line from each object to a number, starting with 1 and continuing in order. Ask children to circle the number that tells how many objects are in each group.

Discuss It How do you know which number tile tells how many objects are in each group?

Practice Counting

Example

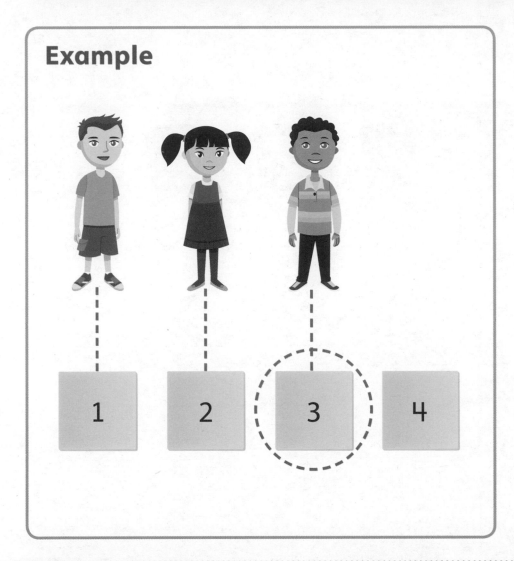

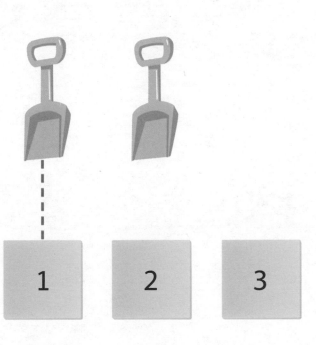

Have children match each object to a tile to find the number of objects. Have children draw a line from each object to a number, starting with 1 and continuing in order. Ask children to circle the number that tells how many objects are in the group.

Lesson 1 Understand Counting   **15**

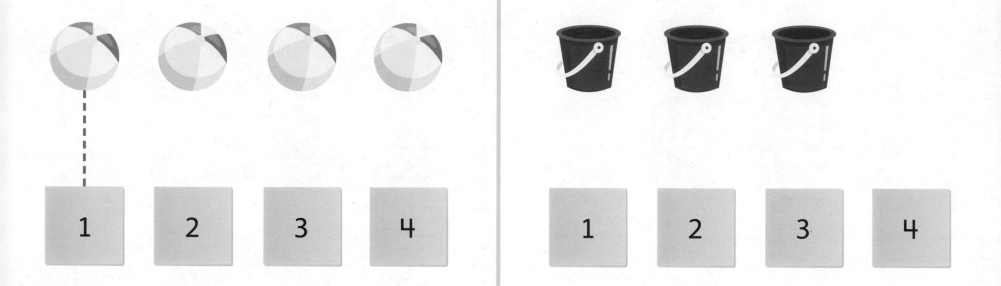

Have children match each object to a tile to find the number of objects.
Have children draw a line from each object to a number, starting with 1 and continuing in order. Ask children to circle the number that tells how many objects are in each group.

16   **Lesson 1** Understand Counting

Refine Ideas About Counting

Apply It

1	2	3	4

1	2	3	4

Have children match each object to a tile to find the number of objects. Have children draw a line from each object to a number, starting with 1. Ask children to circle the number that tells how many objects.

Discuss It How does drawing a line from each girl to a number help you know how many girls there are?

Connect It

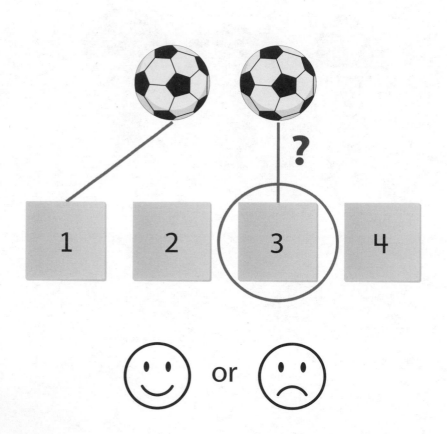

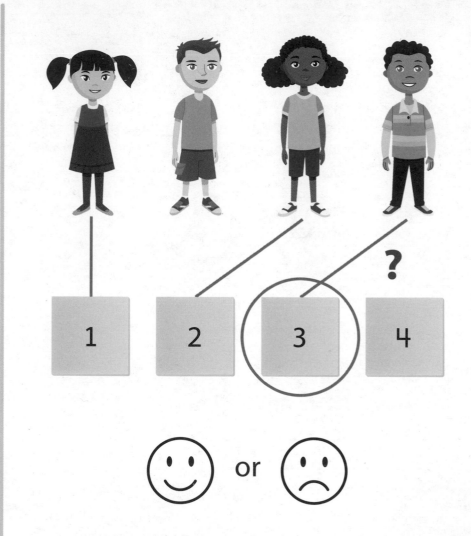

Have children discuss whether the objects are counted correctly or not. Have children color the happy face if the objects are counted correctly or the sad face if they are not. Ask children to describe what is wrong.

Discuss It What is the mistake in counting the soccer balls? What is the mistake in counting the children?

Count and Write to 5

Dear Family,

This week your child is building counting skills with the numbers 1 through 5.

Counting skills include learning to recognize and count groups of 1, 2, 3, 4, and 5 objects. An example of this is finding groups of 1, 2, 3, 4, and 5 objects in pictures and in the classroom. Your child will continue to develop the understanding that when objects are counted, each number is associated with one object and the last number counted tells the total amount in the group. He or she will also continue exploring strategies for keeping track of objects while counting, such as by pointing to or touching each object as it is counted.

This lesson begins to explore the idea that numbers can be represented in various ways. For example, the dots below can be colored in more than one way to show 3.

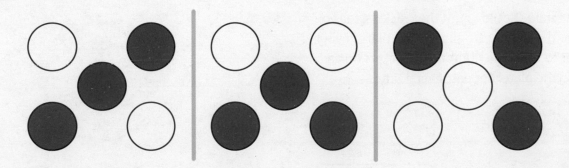

A helpful counting strategy is using fingers to count groups of 5, raising one finger at a time while counting until all 5 fingers on one hand are raised.

Your child will also practice writing the numbers 1, 2, 3, 4, and 5. Working with the numbers 1, 2, 3, 4, and 5 will help your child build a strong foundation for success in math.

Invite your child to share what he or she knows about counting 1, 2, 3, 4, and 5 by doing the following activity together.

Activity Counting 1 Through 5

Do this activity with your child to count.

Materials index cards or slips of paper, pencil, plate, bowl of 7 bite-sized crackers
(or other small objects such as dried beans, pennies, or buttons)

Use index cards or slips of paper to make number cards for the numbers 1 through 5.

- Ask your child to place 1 to 5 crackers on the plate. For example, say: *Show me 2 crackers*. He or she should take that number of crackers from the bowl and place them on the plate. Count the crackers on the plate together to check. Repeat several times with different numbers from 1 to 5.

- Then mix up the number cards and place them facedown in a pile. Your child turns over the top card and places that number of crackers on the plate. Repeat several times.

- Finally, place 1 to 5 crackers on the plate. Your child should count the crackers, tell you how many there are, and then place a matching number card next to the plate. If your child needs an extra challenge, ask him or her to write the number of crackers on an index card or slip of paper and place it next to the plate. Repeat several times.

Explore Counting and Writing to 5

Learning Target

- Understand that the last number name said tells the number of objects counted. The number of objects is the same regardless of their arrangement or the order in which they were counted.

SMP 1, 2, 3, 4, 5, 6

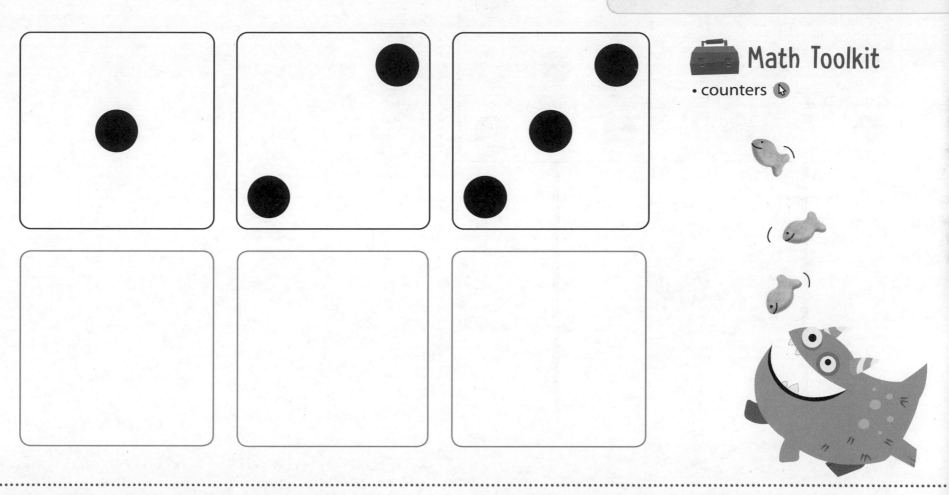

Math Toolkit

- counters

Children make groups of 1, 2, and 3, and practice counting using one-to-one correspondence to find how many are in a group. Introduce the numbers 1, 2, and 3. Discuss activities that 1 child, 2 children, and 3 children might do. Model 1, 2, and 3. Demonstrate counting to show one-to-one correspondence. Then have children draw a picture for 1, 2, and 3.

Connect It

Children explore different arrangements of 4 and 5 using counters.
Introduce 4 using the dot card. Give children counters and have them arrange the counters as shown on the dot card. Repeat using a 5-dot card. Then have children use the counters to show 4 and then 5 in different arrangements.

Prepare for Counting and Writing to 5

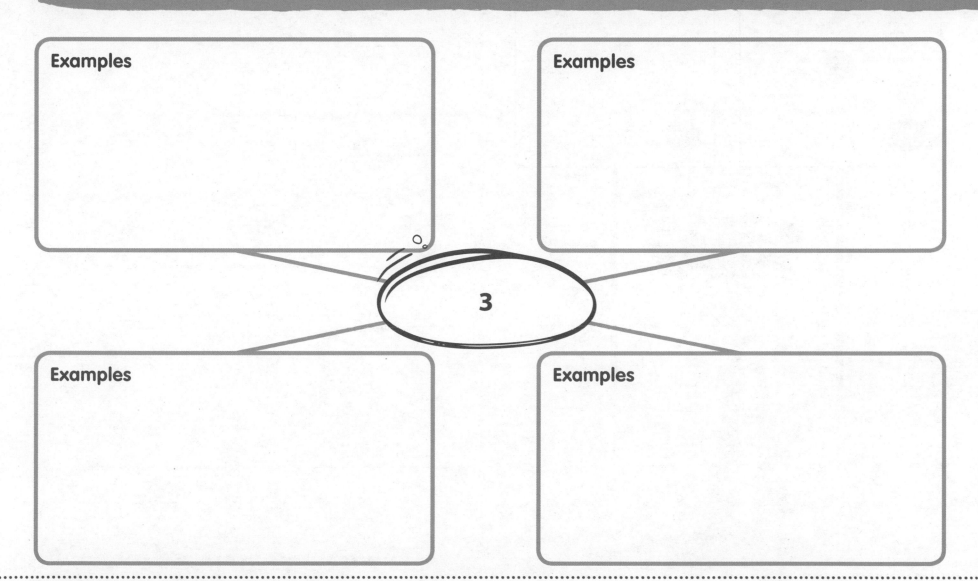

Examples

Examples

3

Examples

Examples

Have children show the meaning of 3. Have children fill in each of the boxes to show the meaning of 3. Tell children that they can use words, numbers, and pictures. Encourage them to show as many ideas as they can.

Have children explore different arrangements of 3 and 2 using small objects. Have children look at the dot card for 3. Give children small objects and have them arrange the objects as shown on the dot card. Then have children use the objects to show 3 in different arrangements. Repeat using a 2-dot card.

Develop Counting and Writing to 5

Encourage children to describe the groups of objects they see in the picture. Ask children to describe the groups based on the size, position, or total number of objects. Have children find at least one group of 1, 2, 3, 4, and 5 related objects.

Discuss It How can you tell if there is 1 pail for each child?

Connect It

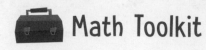 Math Toolkit
• counters

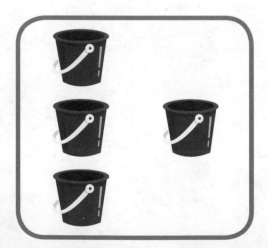

Have children count the number of objects in each group. Then have children draw lines to match groups that show the same number of objects.

Discuss It How can you tell when two groups have the same number of objects?

Practice Counting and Writing to 5

Have children color groups of similar objects. Have children color groups of 1 yellow, groups of 2 red, groups of 3 blue, groups of 4 green, and groups of 5 purple.

Have children count the number of objects in each group. Then have children draw lines to match groups that show the same number of objects.

Develop Counting and Writing to 5

Try It

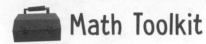 Math Toolkit
- counters
- number cards (1–3)

Have children use counters to make groups of 1, 2, or 3. Give children 5 counters and a set of number cards for 1, 2, and 3. Children place the number cards facedown and then turn one over and use the counters to show that number on the workmat. Repeat.

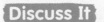 Do you need to use all your counters every time? How do you know when you have the correct number of counters in your group?

Connect It

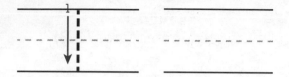 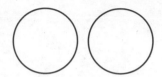

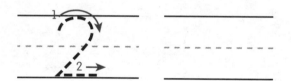 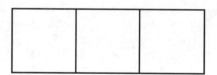 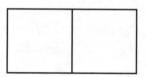

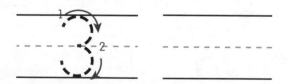  

Have children identify 1, 2, or 3 shapes and write these numbers. Have children trace and write the given numeral. Then ask children to color the group that has that number of shapes.

Discuss It Which pictures show 2? How are the pictures of 2 different from each other?

Practice Counting and Writing to 5

Example

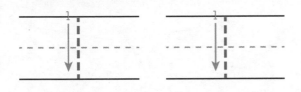

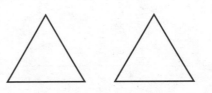

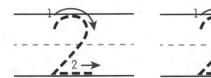

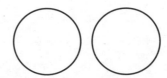

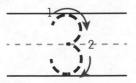

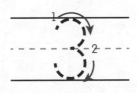

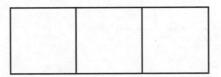

Have children trace the numerals and identify 1, 2, or 3 shapes. Ask
children to trace the two numerals. Then have them color the group that has
that number of shapes.

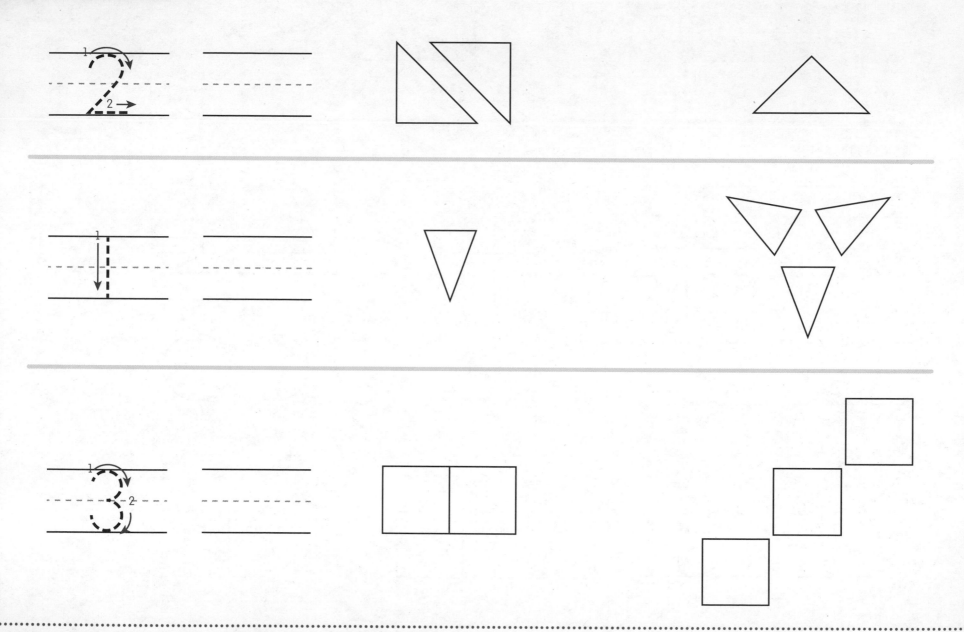

Have children practice writing numerals and identifying 1, 2, or 3 shapes.
Ask children to trace and then write the given numerals. Then have them
color the group that has that number of shapes.

Refine Counting and Writing to 5

Apply It

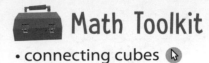
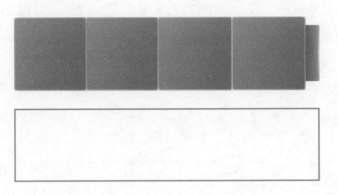

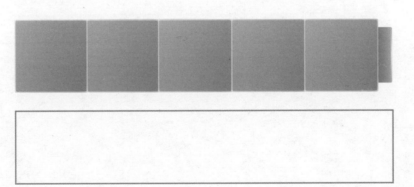

Have children count out groups of 4 and 5 cubes. Give partners 20 cubes, 10 each of two colors. Ask children to make cube trains of 4 cubes. Encourage children to compare against the picture to check. Repeat with trains of 5 cubes.

 **Discuss It** How do you know if you have a 4-cube train or a 5-cube train?

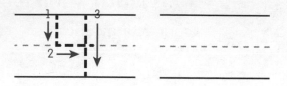

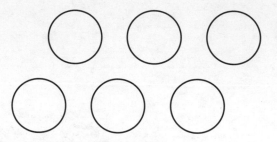

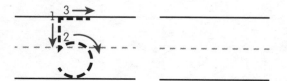

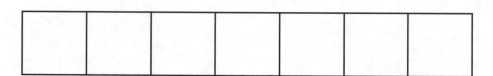

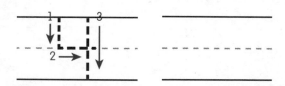

Have children trace and write the numeral and then color or draw 4 or 5. In the first two problems, have children trace and write the numeral, then color that number of shapes. In the last problem, have children trace and write the numeral, then draw the number of shapes.

Discuss It Look at a partner's work. Did you and your partner color the same shapes? How do you know you colored the correct number of shapes?

Practice Counting and Writing to 5

Example

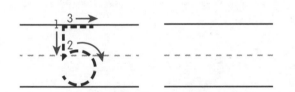

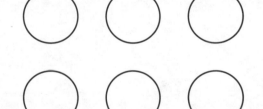

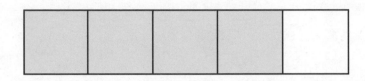

**Have children practice writing the numerals 4 and 5 and counting out 4 or
5 shapes.** Ask children to trace and write the numeral and then color that
number of shapes, as shown in the Example.

4

5

_____

- - - - - - - - - -

_____

_____

- - - - - - - - - -

_____

Have children write the numerals 4 and 5 and draw 4 and 5 objects. On the left, ask children to write the numeral 4 and then draw 4 objects. On the right, ask children to write the numeral 5 and then draw 5 objects.

36   **Lesson 2** Count and Write to 5

Refine Counting and Writing to 5

Apply It

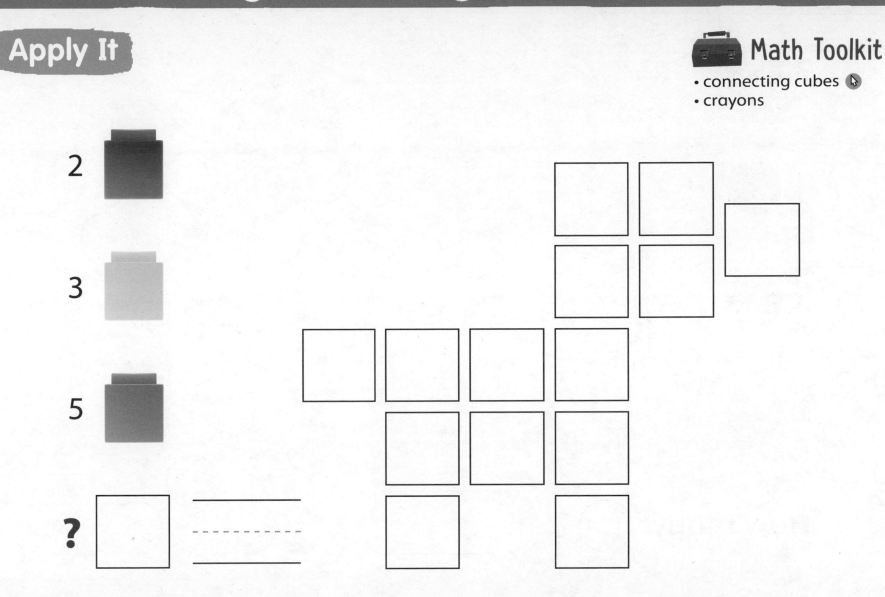

Math Toolkit
- connecting cubes
- crayons

2

3

5

?

Have children practice counting. Give partners 5 red cubes, 5 yellow cubes, and 5 blue cubes. Have children place the appropriate number of each cube on the page. Then ask them to count and write the number of leftover spaces.

Discuss It  How did you find the number of cubes of each color to use?

©Curriculum Associates, LLC   Copying is not permitted.

Lesson 2 Count and Write to 5   **37**

 3

 4

 5

 1

How many 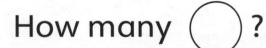 ?

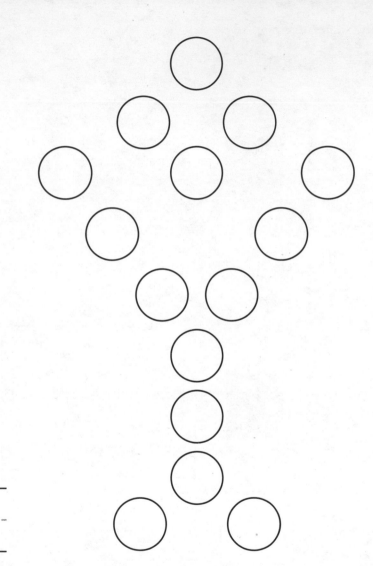

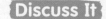

Have children choose independently which circles to color in the given design. Have children color 3 circles orange, 4 red, 5 blue, and 1 yellow. Have children count the number of white circles and write this number.

Discuss It Work with a partner. Where did you color 3 orange? Where did your partner color 3 orange? Are both your pictures right? Why or why not?

Numbers 0 to 5

Dear Family,

This week your child is building counting skills with the number 0.

This skill involves learning to recognize and write the numeral 0 and understand that **zero** represents a group of no objects. For example, when shown a flowerpot with 2 flowers and a flowerpot with no flowers, your child will identify the flowerpot with no flowers as showing 0 flowers.

Your child will also explore how counting numbers represent one **more than** the previous number. He or she will count groups, draw one **more**, and count the group again to find how many are in the group. Your child will see how each number in the counting sequence increases by one.

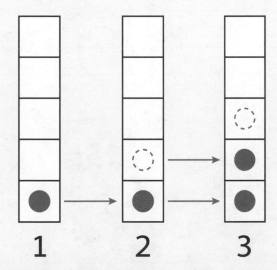

2   0

This lesson also includes practice at recognizing groups of 1 through 5.

Invite your child to share what he or she knows about counting and 0 by doing the following activity together.

Activity Counting 0 to 5

Do this activity with your child to recognize 0 and count.

Materials 6 plastic cups, small sticky notes or labels, and at least 16 objects, such as pencils, crayons, markers, or craft sticks

Tell your child that you are going to work together to organize the objects to show the numbers 0 to 5.

- Have your child write the numbers 0 to 5 on the sticky notes or labels and then place one on each cup.

- Have your child say the numbers to check that they are in the correct order.

- Lay the objects in front of your child. Starting with 0 and then 1, have him or her place the matching number of objects in each cup.

- For numbers 3 to 5, stop your child when he or she has the same amount as the previous number, and ask how many more are needed.

- Starting with 0, have your child count each group of objects to check that each cup holds the correct number.

Explore Numbers 0 to 5

Try It

Learning Target

- Write numbers from 0 to 20. Represent a number of objects with a written numeral 0–20.

SMP 1, 2, 3, 4, 5, 6, 8

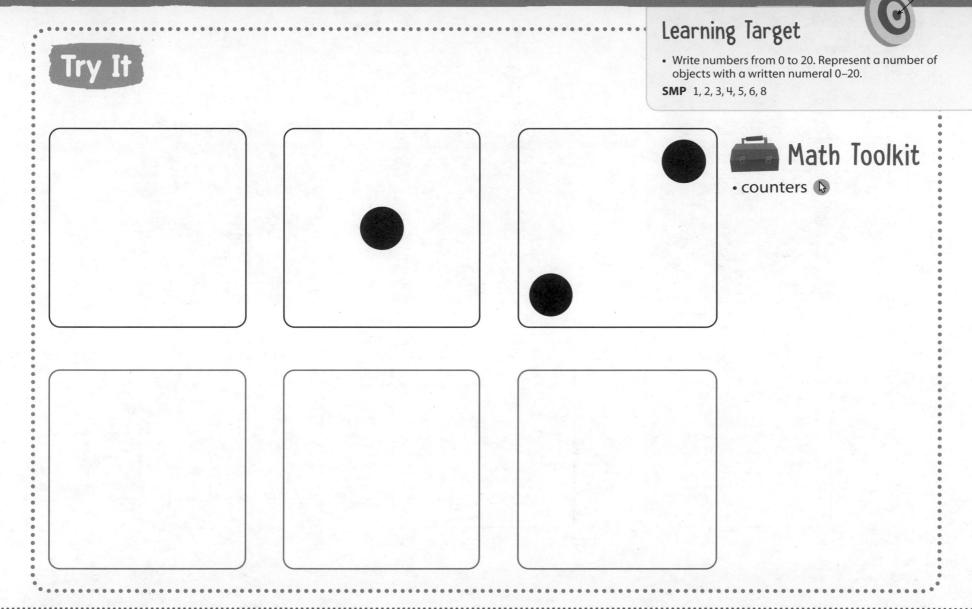

🧰 **Math Toolkit**

- counters

Children make and count groups of 0, 1, 2, 3, 4, and 5. Lay a hoop or circle of rope on the floor. Ask 3 children to stand in the circle, and have children count how many children are in the circle. Repeat with groups of 1, 4, 2, and 5 children in the circle. Last, leave the circle empty and ask how many children are in the circle. Then have children look at the dot cards on the page, count the dots, and draw that number of objects in the box underneath.

Connect It

| 0 | 1 | 2 |

Children use counters, drawings, and fingers to model 0, 1, and 2. Have children place counters in the space below each number to model 0, 1, and 2. Then have children remove the counters and draw dots in the space to show 0, 1, and 2. Point randomly to different cards and ask children to name the number and hold up fingers to show that number. Check that children do not draw dots or hold up fingers for 0.

Prepare for Numbers 0 to 5

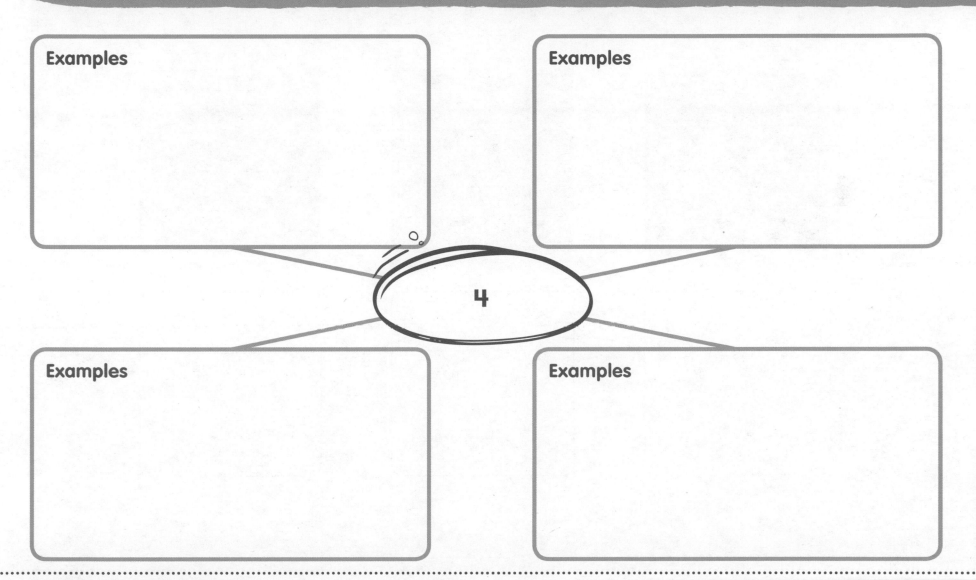

Examples

Examples

4

Examples

Examples

Have children show the meaning of 4. Have children fill in each of the boxes to show the meaning of 4. Tell children that they can use words, numbers, and pictures. Encourage them to show as many ideas as they can.

Have children use drawings and fingers to model 3, 4, and 5. Have children draw dots in the space below each number to show 3, 4, and 5. Then point randomly to different cards and ask children to name the number and hold up fingers to show that number.

Develop Numbers 0 to 5

Have children describe the groups of objects they see in the picture. Ask how many children are sitting on each bench. Have them describe how many birds are in each nest and how many flowers are in each planter. Have them circle the empty planter, bench, and nest.

Discuss It How can you describe how many objects are on an empty bench or in an empty pot?

Connect It

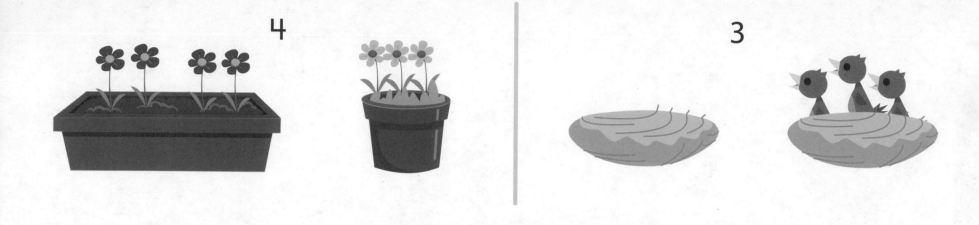

4

3

0

5

Have children describe the pictures. Have children circle the planter with 4 flowers, the nest with 3 birds, the bench with 0 children, and the tree with 5 apples.

Discuss It   How do you know which picture has 0 objects on it or in it?

Practice Numbers 0 to 5

Ask children to find groups of 1, 2, 3, 4, and 5 as well as groups of 0 objects. Make sure children count each object in the group only once.

Have children color the planter with 0 flowers orange, the bench with 0 children brown, and the nest with 0 birds yellow.

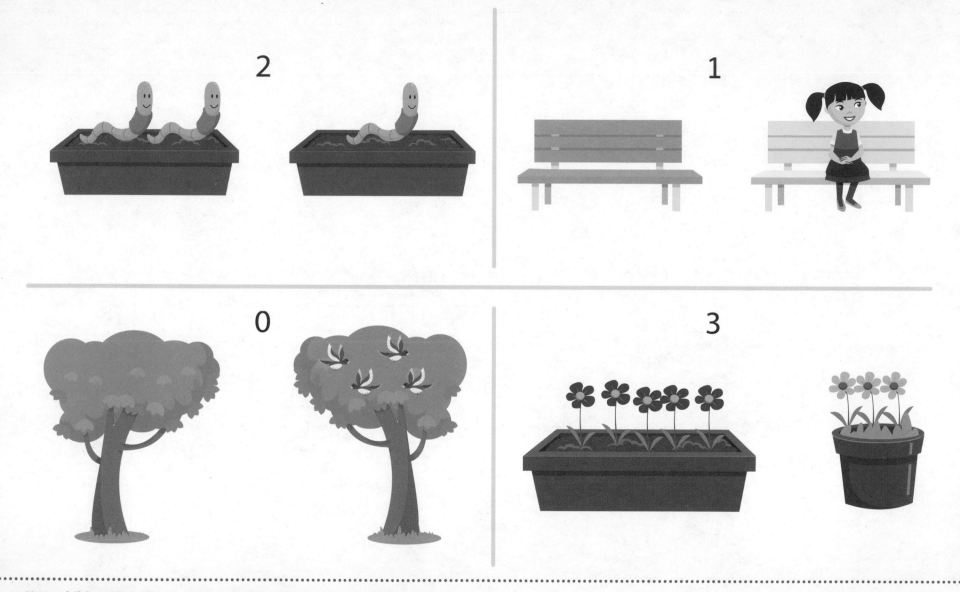

Have children describe the pictures. Ask children to find and point to a group of 1, 2, 3, 4, and 5. Have children circle the planter with 2 worms, the bench with 1 child, the tree with 0 birds, and the planter with 3 flowers.

Develop Numbers 0 to 5

Try It

 Math Toolkit
- counters

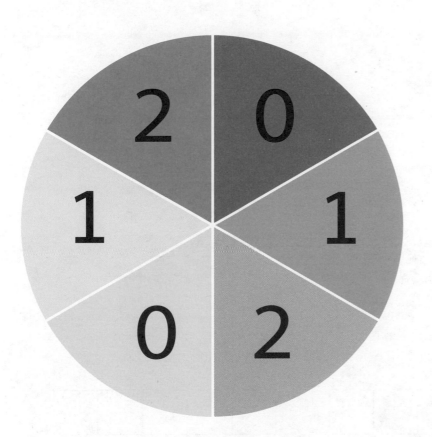

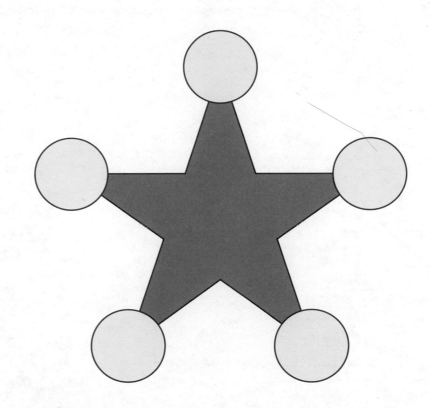

Have children identify and count out 0, 1, and 2. Give children a paper clip, a pencil, and 6 counters each. Explain that 0 means no counters. Children spin the spinner and put that many counters on the points of the star. Repeat until the star has 5 points covered.

Discuss It  Which numbers help you to fill the points of the star? Why?

Connect It

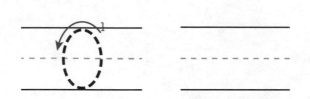

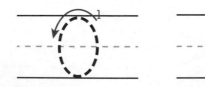

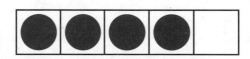

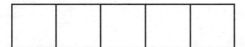

Have children trace and write the numeral 0, read the number aloud, and then find the picture that shows 0. Ask children to circle the picture that shows 0.

Discuss It Look at each picture. How can you tell when a picture shows 0? What numbers do the other pictures show?

Practice Numbers 0 to 5

Example

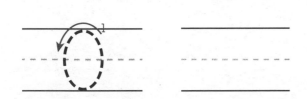  

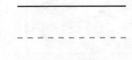  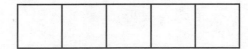

**Have children practice writing the numeral 0 and then find a picture that
shows 0.** Ask children to trace and write the numeral 0 and then circle the
picture that shows 0.

Have children practice writing the numerals 0, 2, and 5 and then find the picture that shows that number. Ask children to trace and write the numerals shown. Then have them circle the picture that shows that number.

Refine Numbers 0 to 5

Apply It

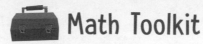

Math Toolkit

• counters

Have children count a set of counters by moving one more each time. Give children 5 counters and have them place the counters in the blue box. Have children count how many are in the group by moving each counter across to the red box as it is counted.

Discuss It How many counters start in the red box? What is happening to the group of counters in the red box as you count them?

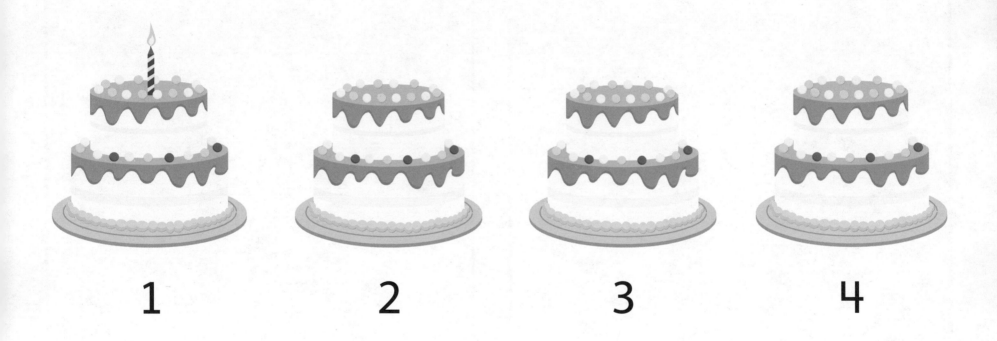

1   2   3   4

Have children draw and count 2, 3, and 4 candles. Say: *When Zoe turned 1, she had 1 candle on her cake. The next year, she turned 2. How many candles should she have on her cake?* Have children draw and count the candles. Repeat for when Zoe turned 3 and 4.

Discuss It Look at each birthday cake, starting with the first one. How can you describe how the number of candles changes each time?

Practice Numbers 0 to 5

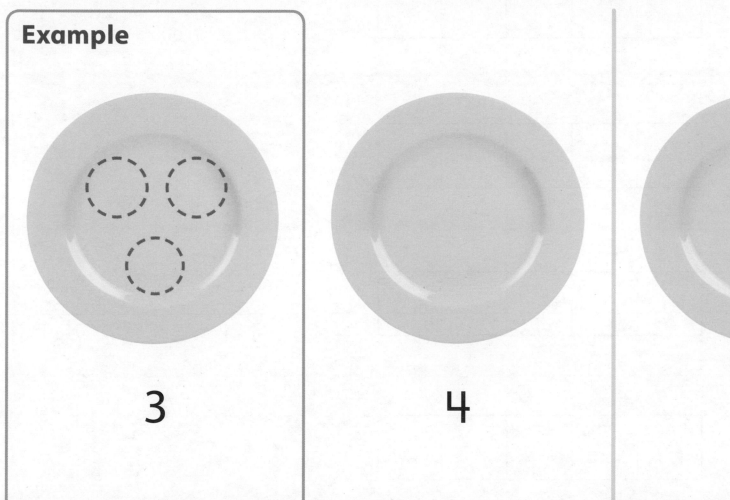

Example

3

4

5

Have children draw one more each time to match the counting numbers. Read the numbers 3, 4, 5 together. Have children draw that number of crackers on each plate. Then have children count and say how many are on each plate. Prompt children to recognize that they have drawn one more each time.

1

2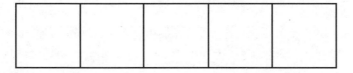

3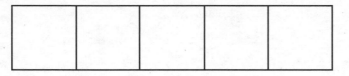

4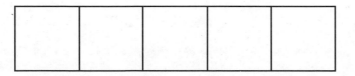

Have children color one more square each time to match the counting numbers. Read the numbers 1, 2, 3, 4 together. Have children color that number of squares in each frame. Then have children count and say how many are in each frame. Prompt children to recognize that they have colored one more each time.

Refine Numbers 0 to 5

Apply It

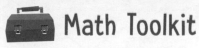 **Math Toolkit**
· connecting cubes

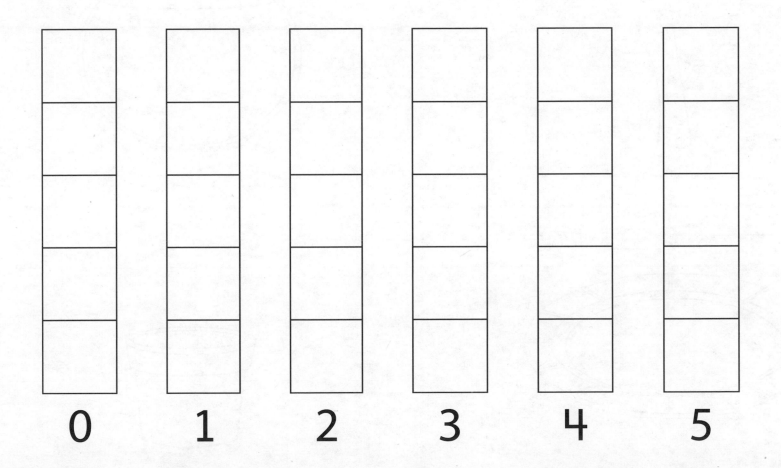

0   1   2   3   4   5

Have children show 0, 1, 2, 3, 4, 5. Give each child 5 cubes. Have children show 1 in the frame labeled 1 by placing 1 cube. Have them slide the cube to the next frame and put on 1 more cube to show the next counting number. Repeat to 5.

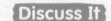 How could you show 0 in the frame? How did you show the next counting number each time?

2

0

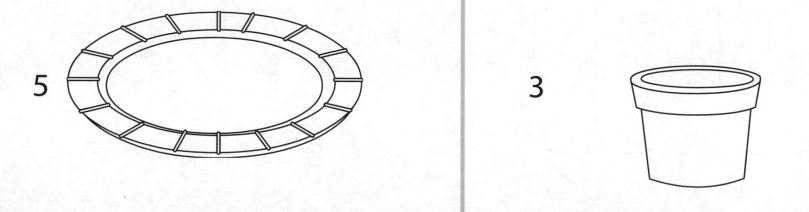

5

3

Have children draw objects to show numbers 0 to 5. Have children draw 2 apples in the tree, 0 fish in the fishbowl, 5 crackers on the plate, and 3 flowers in the flowerpot.

Discuss It How do you know you have drawn the correct number of objects in each picture? How did you show 0 fish in the fishbowl?

Compare Within 5

Dear Family,

This week your child is learning to compare within 5.

The lesson includes **comparing** groups of up to 5 objects. For example, your child may compare a group of 3 blue blocks and a group of 4 green blocks to find that there are more green blocks. Comparing groups of objects to find which has **more** and which has **fewer** helps to prepare your child to **compare numbers** to find which is **greater** and which is **less**. These are important mathematical and real-world skills.

Your child will explore various strategies for comparing, such as lining up the groups of objects being compared in separate rows to see which group has more objects and which group has fewer objects. Another strategy includes crossing out one object from each group of objects until one group has no more to cross out. Or your child may be able to recognize which group has more by just looking at the groups.

5 is more than 4.

Invite your child to share what he or she knows about comparing within 5 by doing the following activity together.

Activity Comparing Within 5

Do this activity with your child to compare within 5.

Materials 2 sets of dot cards for 1–5 (Make by drawing 1 to 5 dots on an index card. There should be 2 cards for each number.)

Tell your child that you are going to practice comparing numbers by playing two games: Go for More and Go for Less.

- To play Go for More, you and your child each get a facedown set of dot cards, shuffled. For each round, you each turn over the card on the top of your pile.

- Your child compares the number of dots on each card and says which card shows more. For example, if your dot card shows 4 dots and your child's shows 2 dots, your child should say: *4 is more than 2*. If the cards show the same number of dots, turn over the next card.

- The person who turned over the dot card showing more gets 1 point. Play until someone gets 5 points.

- Then play Go for Less. In this game, your child says which dot card shows less. For example, your child could say: *2 is less than 4*. This time, the person whose dot card shows less gets 1 point.

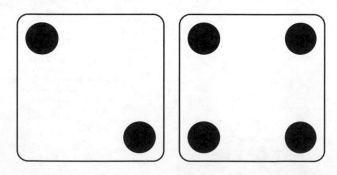

4 is more than 2.

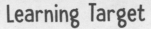
Explore Comparing Within 5

Learning Target

- Identify whether the number of objects in one group is greater than, less than, or equal to the number of objects in another group.

SMP 1, 2, 3, 4, 5, 6

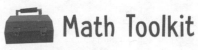 Math Toolkit

- counters

Children discuss ways to find out if two children have the same number of snacks or if one has more. Then they compare groups of counters. Give one child 3 snacks and another child 2 snacks. Ask: *How do we know if* *both children got the same number of snacks?* Discuss ways to compare. Pair children and give each child 1 to 5 counters. Have each child place his or her counters on one of the workmats and then compare to see who has more.

Connect It

Children compare groups of counters to find if they are the same or one has more. Hold up 1 snack in one hand and 3 snacks in the other hand. Have children use counters to model. Ask: *Which hand has more snacks?*

How do you know? Then hold up 2 snacks in each hand. Have children model with counters and compare.

Prepare for Comparing Within 5

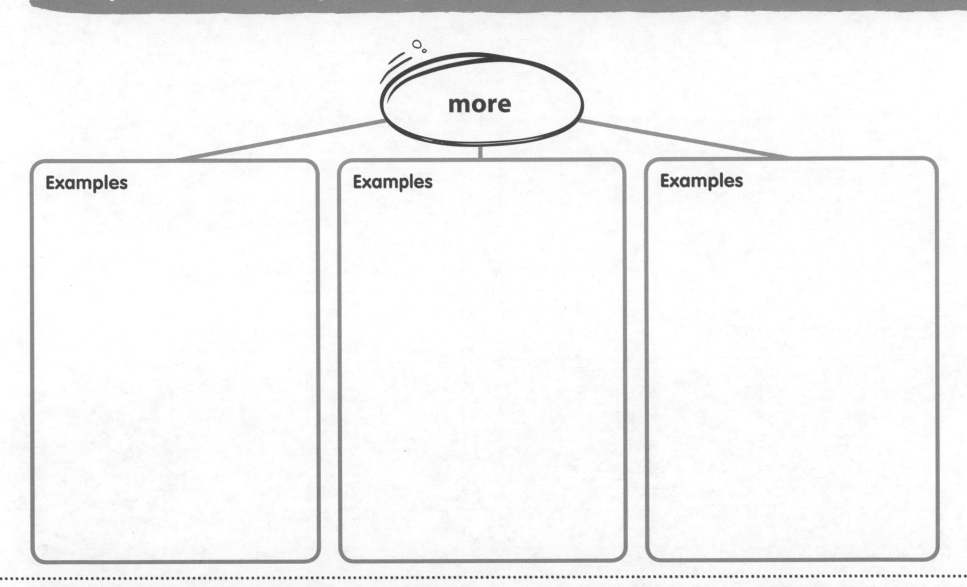

Have children show the meaning of the word *more*. Have children fill in each of the boxes to show the meaning of the word *more*. Tell children that they can use words, numbers, and pictures. Encourage them to show as many ideas as they can.

Children discuss ways to find out whether two groups have the same number of objects or if one has more. Then they compare groups of objects. Give children a group of 3 objects and a group of 4 objects. Ask: *How do we know* *if the two groups have the same?* Discuss ways to compare. Give children up to 10 objects. Have children place some objects on one of the workmats and some on the other workmat and then compare to find which side has more.

Develop Comparing Within 5

Encourage children to talk about the number of objects of various types. Ask children to make comparison statements using *more, less, fewer,* or *the same*. Have them draw lines from each plate to one cup to compare those groups.

Discuss It Do you think there are more than 3 people coming to this party? Why or why not?

Connect It

Have children draw lines to connect objects and circle the group with more. For each problem, ask children to tell which group has more and explain how they know.

Discuss It   How does drawing lines to connect objects help you know which group has more?

Practice Comparing Within 5

Have children find a group of more than 4 similar objects and color those objects green. Then have children find a group of fewer than 4 similar objects and color those objects orange. Ask them to color the rest of the picture using different colors.

Have children draw lines to connect objects and circle the group with more. For each problem, ask children to tell which group has more and explain how they know.

Develop Comparing Within 5

 Try It

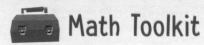 **Math Toolkit**
- counters
- dot cards (2–4)

More   Fewer

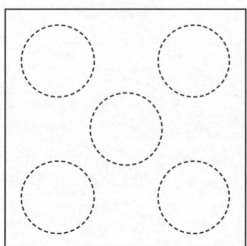   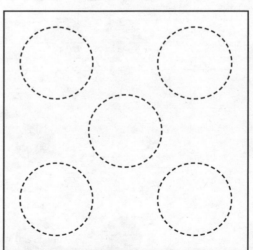

Have children show more than and fewer than the number of dots shown on a dot card. Have children put the dot card in the square at the top of the page. Allow them to decide how many counters to put in the frames to show more and fewer.

Discuss It How did you decide how many to show?

Connect It

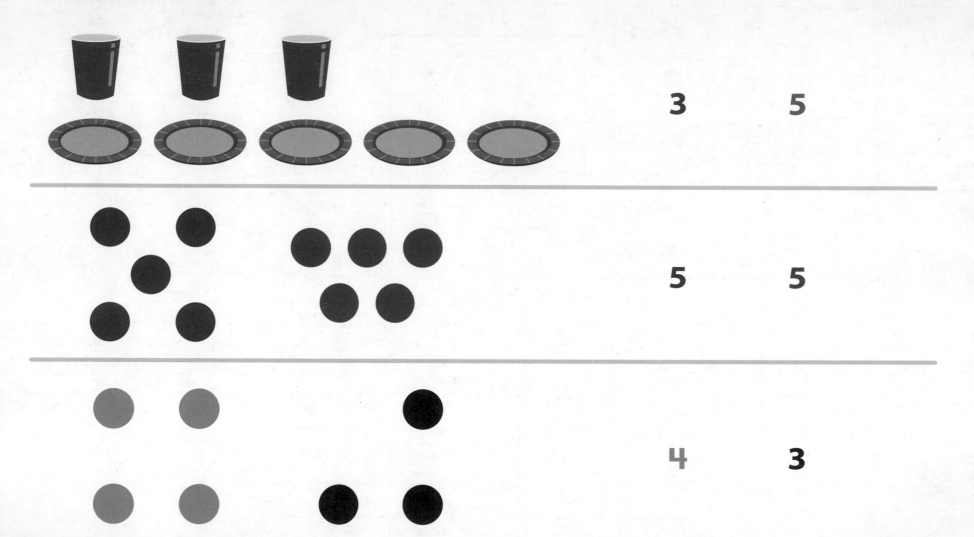

3   5

5   5

4   3

Have children compare two groups of objects and circle the greater number. If the groups have the same number, have children circle both numbers. For each problem, ask children to discuss how they can tell which group has a greater number of objects.

Discuss It What does it mean for two groups to have an equal number of objects?

Practice Comparing Within 5

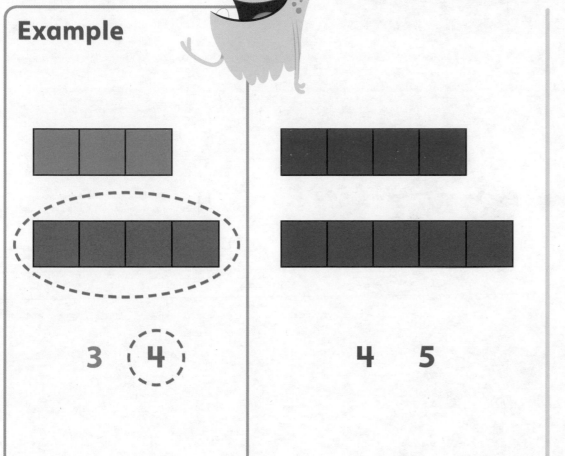

Example

3   (4)

4   5

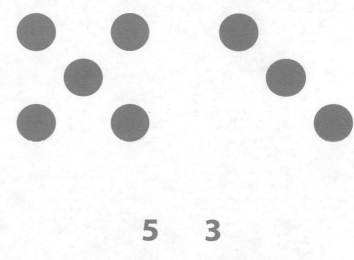

5   3

Have children compare the two groups of shapes and circle the group with more. Then ask children to circle the number that is greater.

0   3

4   4

2   3

Have children compare the two groups of objects and circle the group with fewer. Then ask children to circle the number that is less. If the groups are equal, have children circle both groups and both numbers. For each problem, ask children to explain how they can tell which group has the number that is less.

Refine Comparing Within 5

Apply It

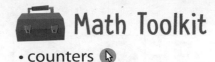 **Math Toolkit**
• counters

Which is greater?

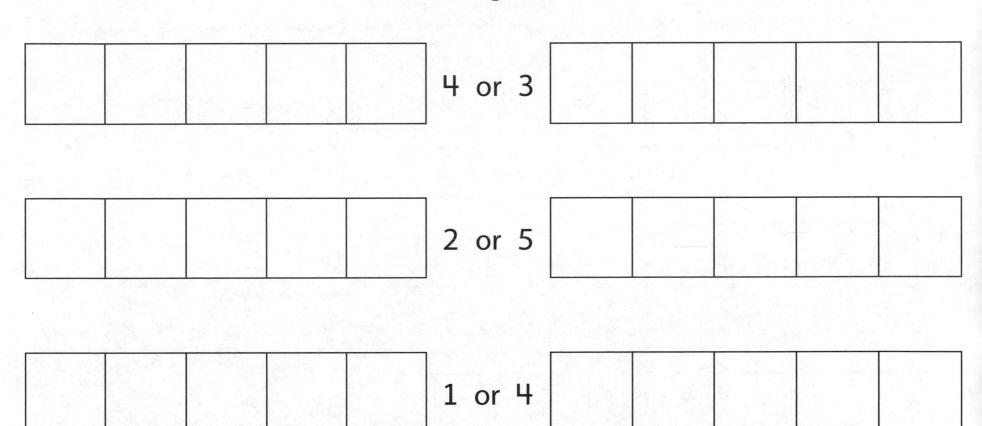

4 or 3

2 or 5

1 or 4

Have children compare numbers. First have them compare numbers and tell which is greater. Have children represent each number with counters to check their comparisons. For each problem, have them circle the number that is greater.

 **Discuss It** How did using counters in the frames help you check your comparisons?

Which is less?

_____

- - - - - - -   or   4

_____

_____

- - - - - - -   or   5

_____

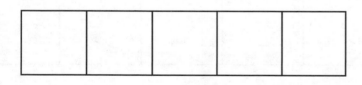

_____

- - - - - - -   or   2

_____

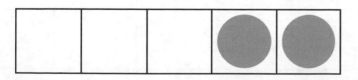

_____

- - - - - - -   or   3

_____

Have children count and write how many counters are shown. Ask them to compare that number with the number on the right and circle the one that is less. For each problem, ask children to discuss how they can tell which is less.

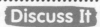 Look at each group of counters. Which group of counters has less than any of the others? How can you be sure?

Practice Comparing Within 5

Example

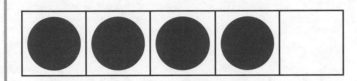

Which is greater?

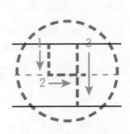 or 1

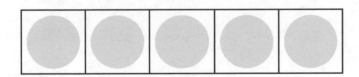

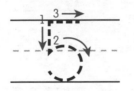 or 2

_____ or 5

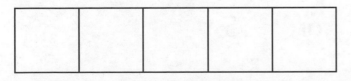

_____ or 3

Have children count and write how many counters are shown. Ask children to compare the number they wrote with the number on the right. Have them circle the number that is greater, as shown in the Example.

Which is less?

_____
- - - - - - - -   or   2
_____

_____
- - - - - - - -   or   0
_____

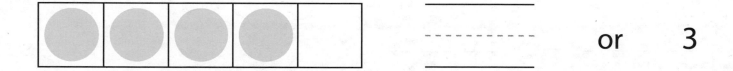

_____
- - - - - - - -   or   3
_____

_____
- - - - - - - -   or   5
_____

Have children count and write how many counters are shown. Ask children to compare the number they wrote with the number on the right. Have them circle the number that is less.

76   **Lesson 4** Compare Within 5

Refine Comparing Within 5

Apply It

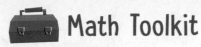 **Math Toolkit**
- number cubes (labeled 0–5)

Greater

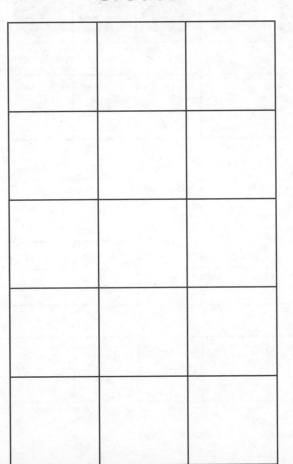

Less

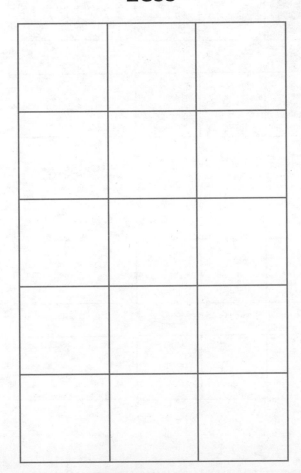

Have children compare numbers and fill grids. Give partners two 0–5 number cubes. Have them roll both cubes and figure out which number is greater. Color that many spaces in the red grid. Color the lesser number of spaces in the blue grid. Repeat until one grid is full.

Discuss It Did you know which color would fill up first? Will that color fill up first every time? Why or why not?

Draw more.

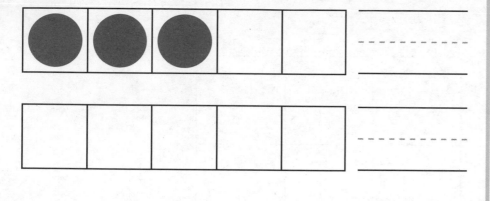

Draw fewer.

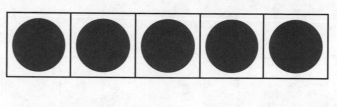

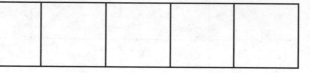

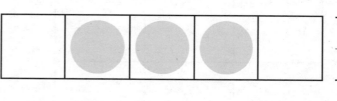

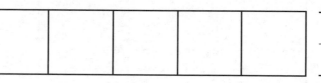

Have children draw more or fewer counters than those shown in the top 5-frame of each pair. Have children count and write the given number of counters. Allow children to decide how many counters to draw to show more or fewer.

Discuss It  How can you be sure you drew more?
How can you be sure you drew fewer?

Make 3, 4, and 5

Dear Family,

This week your child is learning to find the numbers that make 3, 4, and 5.

Numbers can be thought of as being made up of combinations of other numbers. For example, 4 is made up of 1 and 3, 2 and 2, or 3 and 1. Thinking of numbers this way will help your child prepare for adding and subtracting numbers. For example, knowing that 1 and 3 make 4 lays the foundation for knowing $1 + 3 = 4$. The ways to make 3, 4, and 5 are listed below.

Ways to Make 3	Ways to Make 4	Ways to Make 5
1 and 2	1 and 3	1 and 4
2 and 1	2 and 2	2 and 3
	3 and 1	3 and 2
		4 and 1

In class, your child will explore ways to make 3, 4, and 5 using pictures and objects. For example, putting together connecting cubes of different colors helps to visualize the ways to make 4, as shown below.

1 and 3

4

Invite your child to share what he or she knows about making 3, 4, and 5 by doing the following activity together.

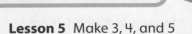

Activity Making 3, 4, and 5

Do this activity with your child to explore making 3, 4, and 5.

Materials 5 small objects (such as pasta shapes, dried beans, cereal pieces, buttons, or paper clips), paper plate or sheet of paper

• Draw a line down the center of a paper plate or sheet of paper.

• Give your child 3 small objects. Have your child count the objects and then place them on the plate or paper.

• Show your child how to place the objects on both sides of the line to show a way to make 3. Encourage him or her to tell how the objects make 3. For example, if 1 object is on the left and 2 objects are on the right, your child might say: *1 and 2 make 3*. Then have your child rearrange the objects to show another way to make 3. If there are 2 objects on the left and 1 on the right, he or she might say: *2 and 1 make 3*.

• Repeat the activity, starting with 4 objects and then 5 objects. Try to find and describe all the ways to make each number.

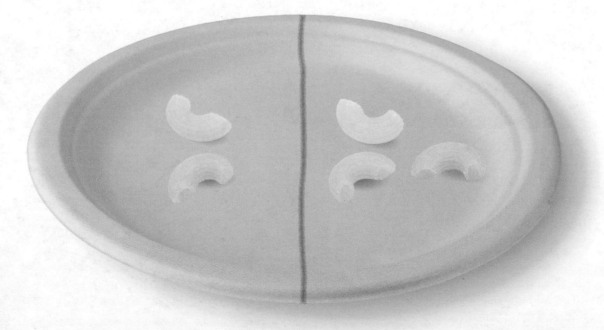

Explore Making 3, 4, and 5

Try It

Learning Targets

- Decompose numbers less than or equal to 10 into pairs in more than one way, and record each decomposition by a drawing or equation.
- Fluently add and subtract within 5.

SMP 1, 2, 3, 4, 5, 6, 7

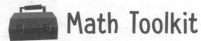 Math Toolkit

- counters 🖑
- two-color counters 🖑
- crayons

Have children count groups of 5 and use counters as a standard for finding groups of 5. Give each child 5 crayons and ask: *How many crayons are there?* Have children make different groups of 5 by arranging the crayons in different ways. Then give children 5 counters. Have children practice one-to-one correspondence by gathering groups of 5 objects in the classroom and placing one counter on each object to verify.

Connect It

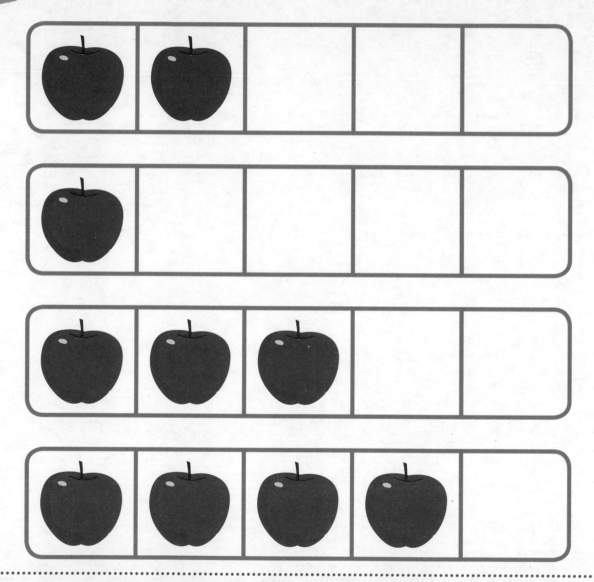

Have children model problems using counters. Pose a problem:
I have 2 red apples. How many yellow apples should I buy to have 5 apples?

Then have children use counters to solve the problem. Pose more problems starting with 1, 3, and 4 red apples. Have children use counters to solve.

Prepare for Making 3, 4, and 5

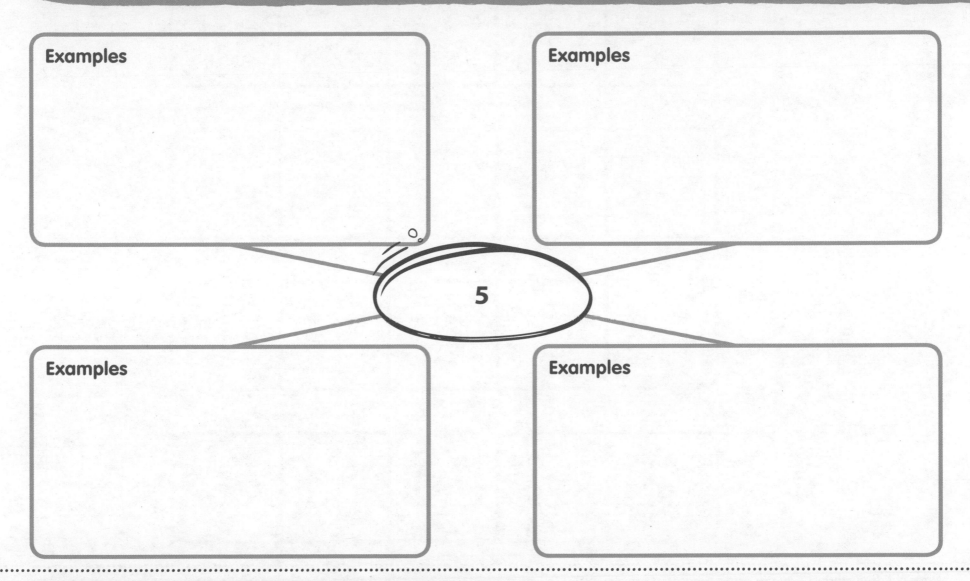

Examples

Examples

5

Examples

Examples

Have children show the meaning of 5. Have children fill in each of the boxes to show the meaning of 5. Tell children that they can use words, numbers, and pictures. Encourage them to show as many ideas as they can.

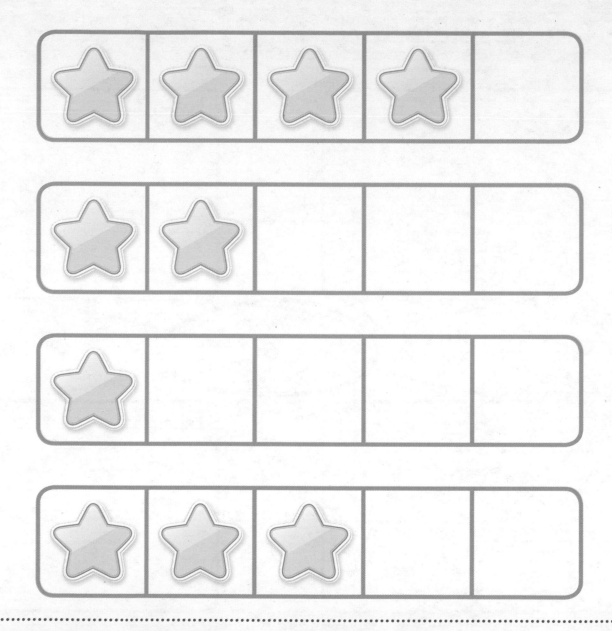

Have children model problems using counters. Pose a problem: *I have 4 star stickers. How many moon stickers should I buy to have 5 stickers?* Then have children use counters or small objects to solve the problem. Pose more problems starting with 2, 1, and 3 star stickers. Have children use counters or small objects to solve.

84   **Lesson 5** Make 3, 4, and 5

Develop Making 3, 4, and 5

Encourage children to talk about each train. Ask how many cars each train has, how many are yellow, and how many are blue. Discuss any patterns they may see. Have children use yellow and blue crayons to show another way to make a train with 5 cars.

Discuss It What is the same about each group of train cars? What is different?

Connect It

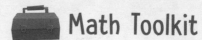 **Math Toolkit**
- two-color counters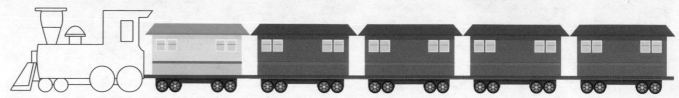
- crayons

 3

 4

 5

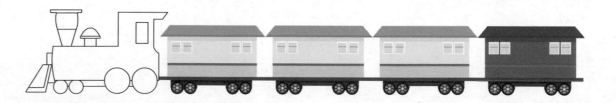

Have children draw lines to match each number to a group of train cars that shows a way to make that number. For each group, have children say how many of each color car makes the total number. For example, 2 yellow and 1 blue make 3.

 **Discuss It** How do you know how many cars are in each train? How do you know how many of each color car are in each train?

Practice Making 3, 4, and 5

Have children use green to color 1 car on the top train, 2 cars on the second train, and 3 cars on the third train. Have them color the rest of the cars in those trains purple. Ask children to color the bottom train green and purple to show another way to make a train with 5 cars. Encourage children to describe the trains with statements such as: *This train has 1 green car and 2 purple cars. 1 and 2 make 3.*

Have children draw lines to match each number to a group of train cars that shows a way to make that number. Have children describe how each number is made. For example, children might say: *1 and 2 make 3*.

Develop Making 3, 4, and 5

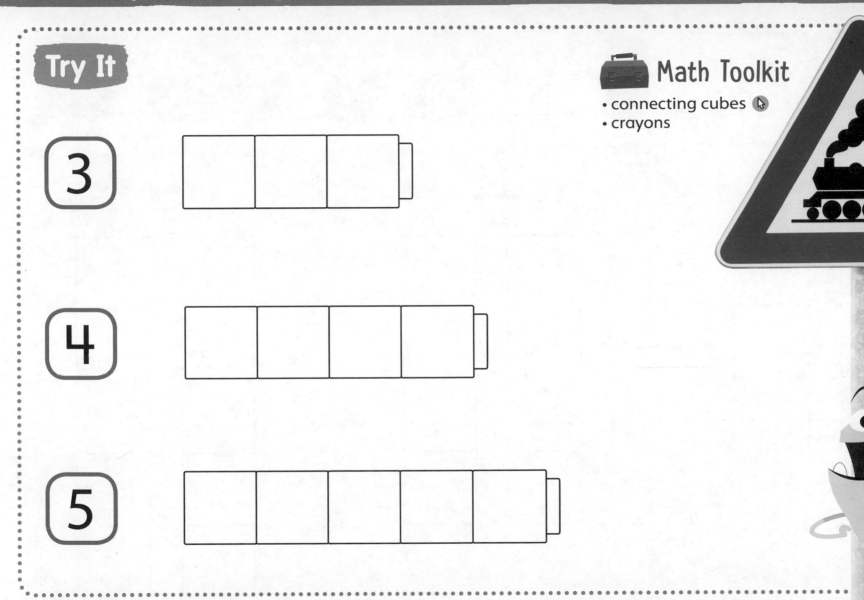

Try It

3

4

5

Math Toolkit
- connecting cubes
- crayons

Have children use cubes to make a two-color train of 3, 4, or 5. Give children cubes, 9 of one color and 9 of another color. Ask children to use both colors to make cube trains to total 3, 4, and 5 and lay them on the mat next to the correct total.

Discuss It Is there more than one way to make each total?

Connect It

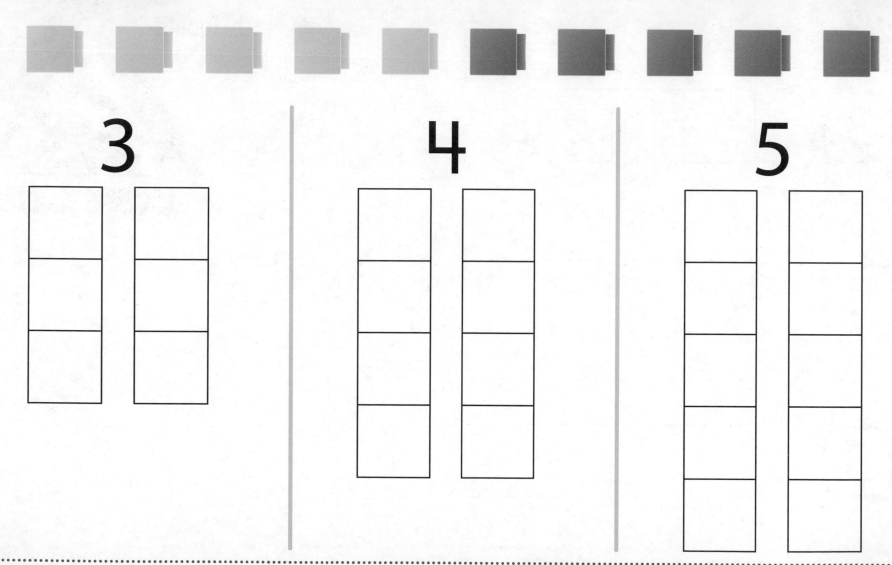

3

4

5

Ask children to build cube trains of 3, 4, and 5 and then record their work by coloring the boxes. Model one way to make a train of 3, and then have children make 3 a different way. Ask children to also show two ways to make 4 and 5.

Discuss It Work with a partner. Tell how many of each color you used to build 3. Did you use the same number of each color? Did you use the same number of cubes?

Practice Making 3, 4, and 5

Example

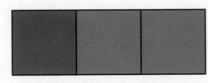

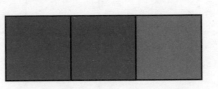

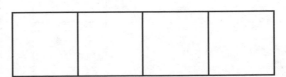

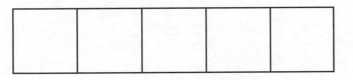

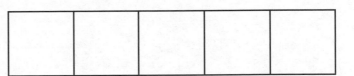

Have children use two colors to show different ways to make the number next to each problem. In the Example problem, point out to children that the first group of boxes shows that 1 and 2 make 3 and the second group of boxes shows that 2 and 1 make 3. Then have children use red and blue crayons to show different ways to make 4 and 5.

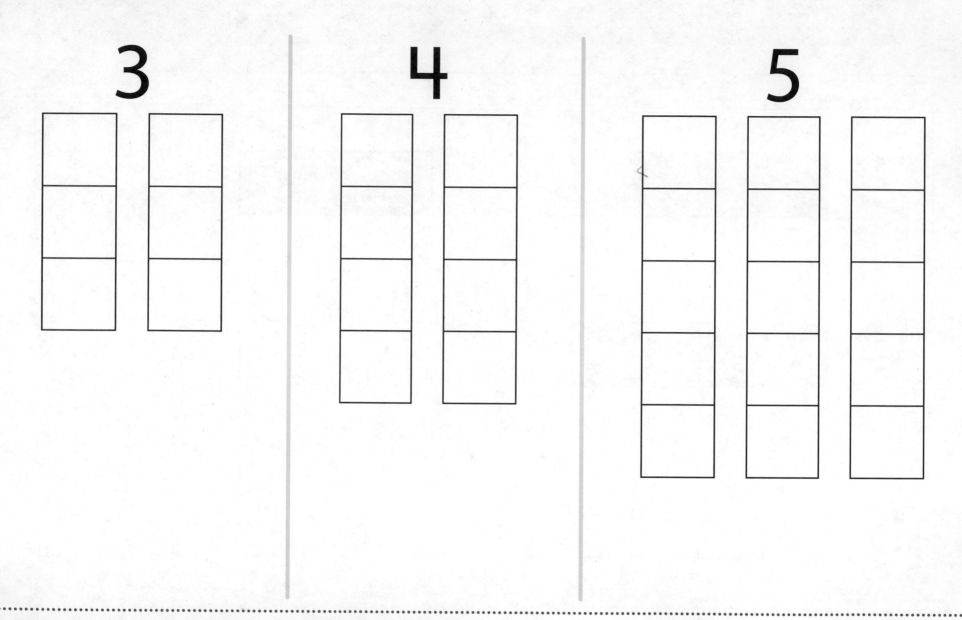

Have children use two colors of crayons to show different ways to make 3, 4, and 5. In the first two problems, have children show two different ways to make 3 and 4. In the last problem, have children show three different ways to make 5.

92   **Lesson 5** Make 3, 4, and 5

Refine Making 3, 4, and 5

Apply It

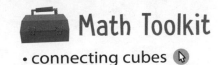 Math Toolkit

• connecting cubes

| 3 | 4 | 5 |

Have children add to a tower to make a total of 3, 4, or 5. Give children cubes to build towers of 1, 2, and 3 and place one tower on each square at random. Ask children how many cubes they need to add to each tower to make the total given in the square.

Discuss It How do you know when you have the correct number of cubes in your tower? How did you find how many more cubes you needed?

Lesson 5 Make 3, 4, and 5   **93**

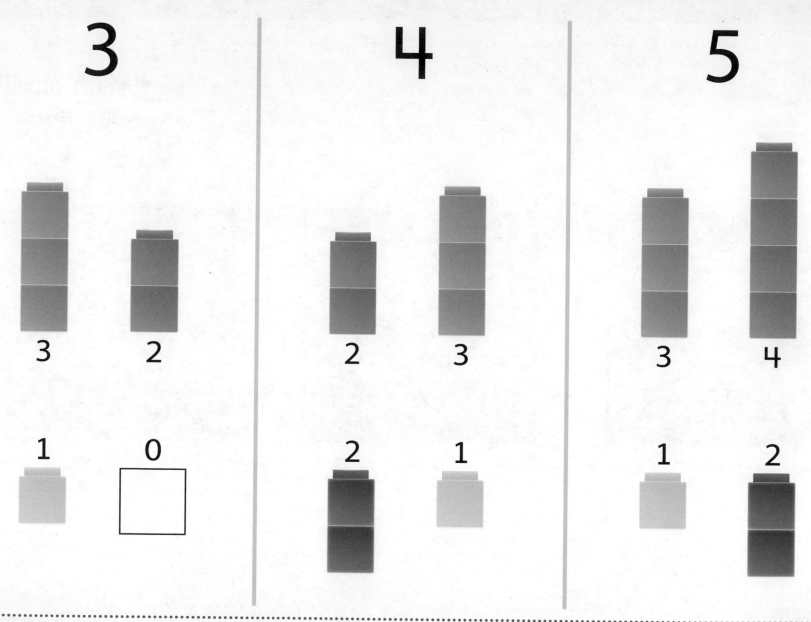

Have children match the pieces on the top to the pieces on the bottom to make trains of 3, 4, and 5. Point out to children that the empty box shows zero cubes. Discuss how many of each color were used, and model other number pairs to make each target number.

Discuss It Can you think of other ways to make 4?

Practice Making 3, 4, and 5

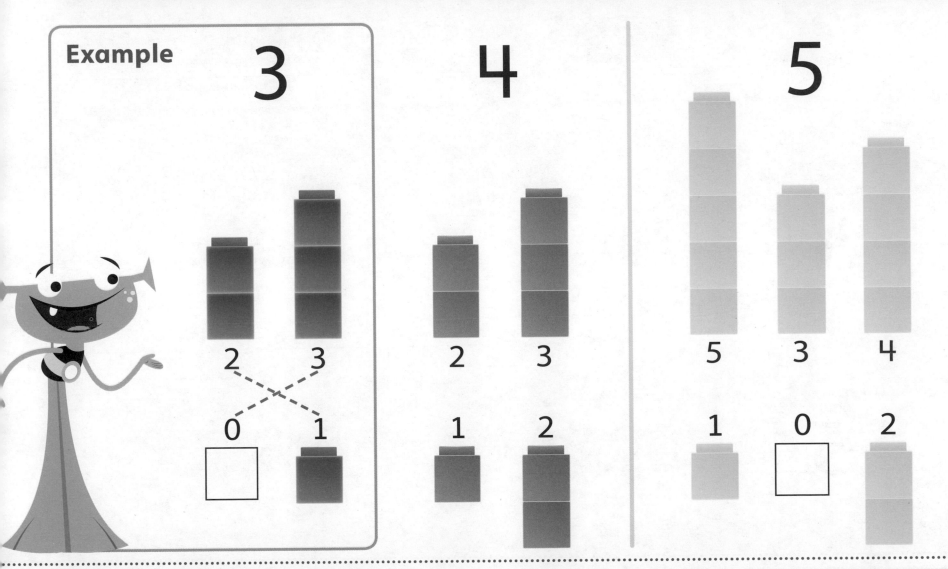

Example

3

2   3

0   1

4

2   3

1   2

5

5   3   4

1   0   2

Have children draw lines to match the cubes on the top to the cubes on the bottom to make cube trains of 3, 4, and 5. Point out to children that in the Example problem, the empty box shows zero cubes. Have children name the number pairs that make each target number. For example, to name the number pairs in the Example problem, children might say: *2 and 1 make 3; 3 and 0 make 3.*

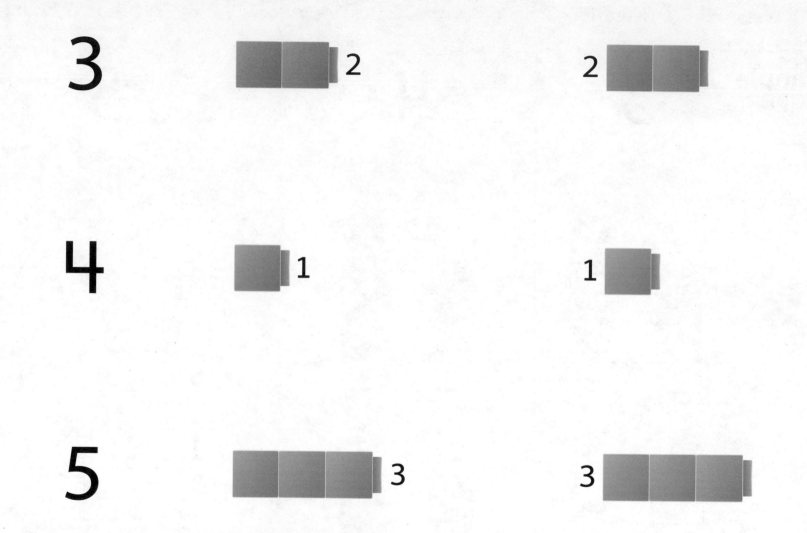

3   2   2

4   1   1

5   3   3

Have children draw lines to match the cubes on the left to the cubes on the right to make trains of 3, 4, and 5. Have children name the number pairs used to make each target number.

Refine Making 3, 4, and 5

Apply It

Make 5.

 Math Toolkit
- two-color counters
- connecting cubes
- crayons

Have children find different ways to make 5 using counters. Give children 5 two-color counters. Ask them to use the counters to show different ways to make 5. Children will choose how many of each color to use.

 How many yellow counters would you need if you used 5 red counters to make 5? Can you make 5 with the same number of red and yellow counters?

Draw 3.

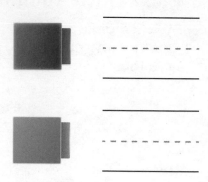

Draw 5.

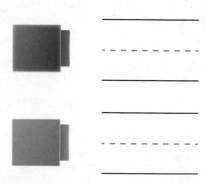

Have children use red and blue cubes to make trains with 3 cubes and then 5 cubes and then, using red and blue, draw a picture to show their trains. Develop children's problem-solving skills by allowing them to decide how many of each color to use.

 How many of each color did you use to build 5? Are there other ways you could build 5 using different numbers of red and blue cubes?

Self Reflection

Show What You Learned

Have children draw to show what they learned about numbers 0–5.
Prompt children to reflect on their learning by posing questions such as:

What do you know how to do well? What math could you use in your everyday life?
What is a question you still have?

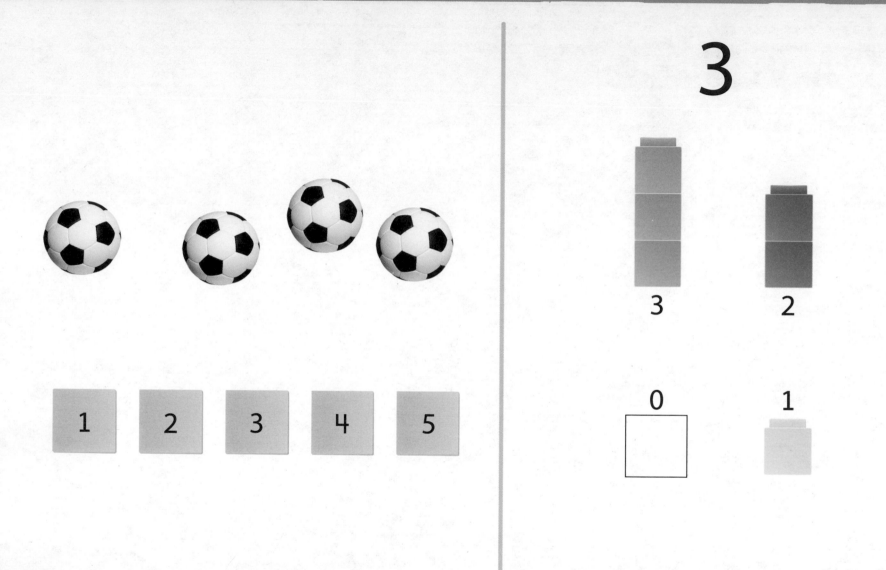

3

3   2

0   1

1   2   3   4   5

For the problem on the left, have children draw a line from each object to a number, starting with 1. Ask children to circle the number that tells how many objects. After children circle the number, have them say how many objects there are, for instance: *There are 4 balls.* For the problem on the right, have children draw lines to match the cubes on the top to the cubes on the bottom to show how to make cube trains of 3. Have children name the number pairs that make the target number, 3.

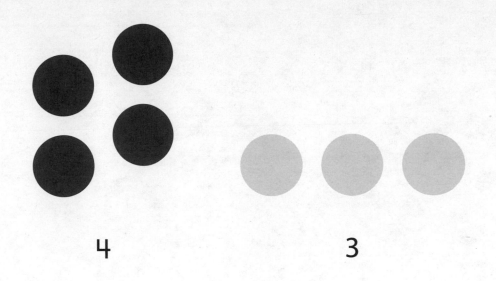

4   3

For the top problem, have children compare groups. Have children circle the number that is less. For the bottom problem, have children draw 3 fish in the fishbowl.

2

_____

_ _ _ _ _

_____

5

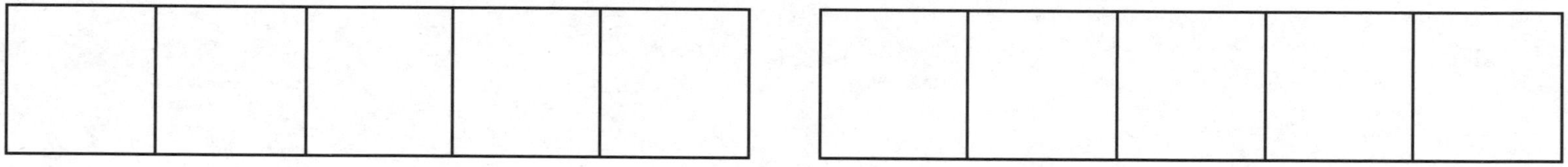

| | | | | | | | | | | |

For the top problem, have children read the given number and look at the group of dolphins. Then have children write that number. For the bottom problem, have children use two colors of crayons to show two different ways to make 5. Then have children name the number pairs.

Show What You Know

Have children draw to show what they know about numbers 6–10. Tell children that after they have completed the unit, they will draw to show what they learned.

Build Your Vocabulary

My Math Words

Ana   Sanza

more than

Ana has   Sanza.

less than

Pete   Mary

more than

Pete has   Mary.

less than

Mary   Pete

more than

Mary has   Pete.

less than

Sanza   Ana

more than

Sanza has   Ana.

less than

Say: Ana, Sanza, Pete, and Mary are all sharing juice. They each poured some into their cup. Have children talk to their partner and use the phrases *more than* and *less than* to describe the amount of juice in each child's cup.

Then have children circle the phrase that makes more sense for each scenario.

Count and Write to 10

Dear Family,

This week your child is building counting skills with numbers up to 10.

The lesson includes practice with counting up to 10 objects. Strategies for keeping track of what has been counted remain important, especially when counting these larger groups. For example, touching or pointing to each object or marking each object in a picture as it is counted are ways to ensure that no items have been missed.

Building on earlier lessons, your child will explore how numbers **6, 7, 8, 9,** and **10** relate to other numbers. For example, the pictures below show how the numbers 6 through 10 visually relate to 5 using fingers or counters. Understanding these numbers as 5 and some more prepares your child for addition concepts and for thinking about these numbers as sums of other numbers.

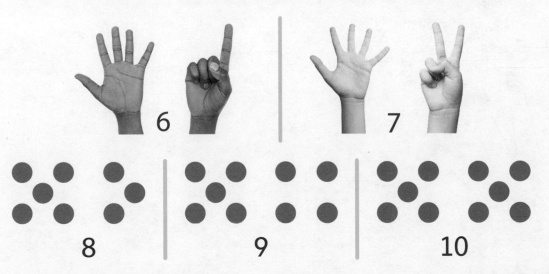

Invite your child to share what he or she knows about counting to 10 by doing the following activity together.

Activity Counting to 10

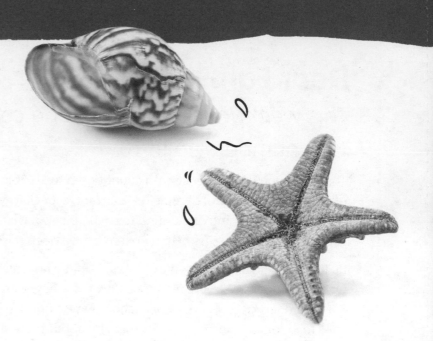

Do this activity with your child to explore counting to 10.

Materials 10 small objects (such as buttons, dried beans, or cereal), dot cube (or homemade number cards 1–6), paper, pencil

Trace your child's two hands on a sheet of paper. Then have your child use the hand picture to do the following activity.

- Roll a dot cube (or turn over a number card) and count out that number of buttons. Place 1 button on each finger.

- Keep rolling and placing buttons until you get to 10—when all fingers are covered. Make sure to stop when you get to 10, no matter what number you rolled. Repeat the activity several times.

- You may want to have your child count the covered fingers to emphasize the relationship between two hands and the number 10.

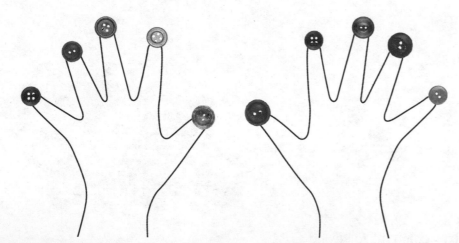

In addition to doing the above activity, practice counting 1 to 10 objects with your child whenever you can. For example, encourage your child to count spoons, apples, crackers, buttons, books, stairs, etc.

Explore Counting and Writing to 10

Learning Target

- Count to answer "how many?" questions about as many as 20 things arranged in a line, a rectangular array, or a circle, or as many as 10 things in a scattered configuration; given a number from 1–20, count out that many objects.

SMP 1, 2, 3, 4, 5, 6, 7

 Math Toolkit

- counters

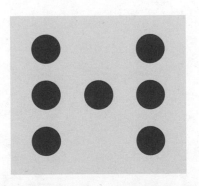

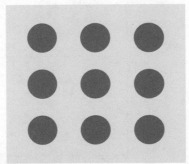

Have children form groups of 6, 7, 8, and 9. Review numbers 1 to 5 using dot cards, and then display the dot card for 6. Give 6 children paper plates and have them use the plates to make an arrangement of 6 on the floor. Repeat, having other groups of 6 children make different arrangements. Then have children use counters to make arrangements of 6 on the workmat, counting to check that each arrangement shows 6. Repeat with 7, 8, and 9 counters.

Connect It

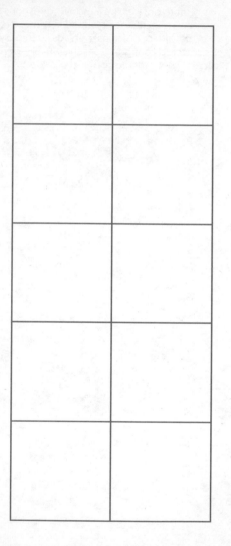

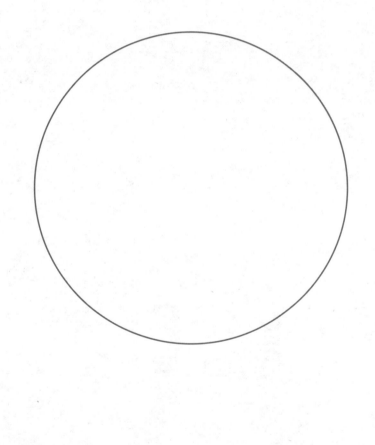

Children explore visual images of 10. Children place 5 counters in a column of the 10-frame. Then they add counters one at a time to fill the frame, counting to verify each time. Next, they move the counters to be around the edge of the circle. Ask: *How do you count objects in a circle?*

Prepare for Counting and Writing to 10

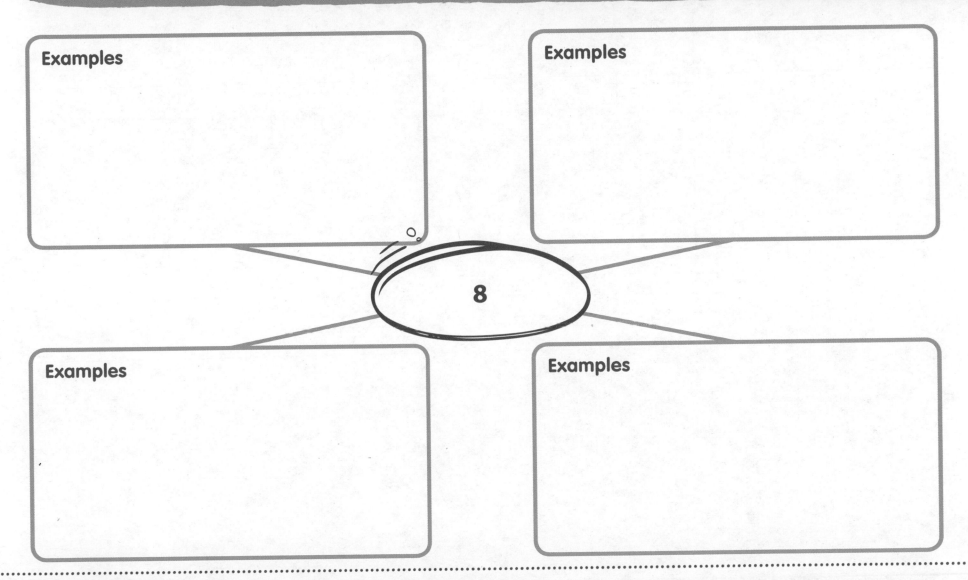

Examples

Examples

8

Examples

Examples

Have children show the meaning of 8. Have children fill in each of the boxes to show the meaning of 8. Tell children that they can use words, numbers, and pictures. Encourage them to show as many ideas as they can.

Children explore visual images of 8. Have children place 8 small objects on the 10-frame, one at a time, counting to verify each time.

Next, they move the objects to be around the edge of the circle. Ask: *How do you count objects in a circle?*

110 **Lesson 6** Count and Write to 10

Develop Counting and Writing to 10

Encourage children to describe groups of 6, 7, 8, 9, and 10 they find in the picture. Discuss other size groups as well and note number pairs for 10, such as 4 large bubbles and 6 small bubbles. Have children circle a group of 10.

Discuss It Work with a partner. Can you find groups that have the same number? How can you tell?

Connect It

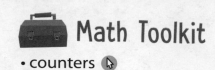 **Math Toolkit**
• counters

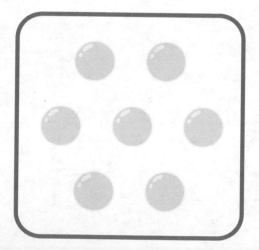

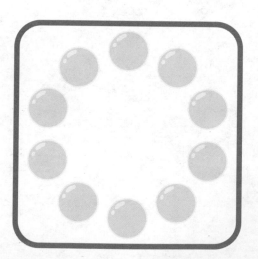

Have children count the number of objects in each group. Then have children draw lines to match groups that show the same number of objects.

 How did you keep track of which objects you counted?

Name: _____

Practice Counting and Writing to 10

Have children count groups of 6, 7, 8, 9, and 10. Have children color groups of 6 red, groups of 7 blue, groups of 8 green, groups of 9 yellow, and groups of 10 purple.

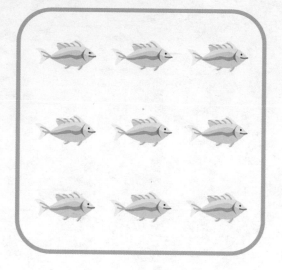

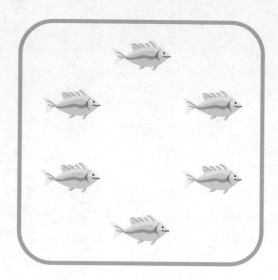

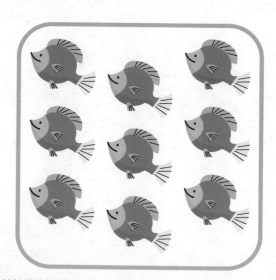

Have children count the number of fish in each group. Then have children draw lines to match groups that show the same number of fish.

Develop Counting and Writing to 10

 **Try It**

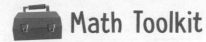 **Math Toolkit**

- counters
- dot cards (6–8)

Have children use counters to make groups of 6, 7, or 8. Give children 10 counters and a set of dot cards for 6, 7, and 8. Children place the dot cards facedown and then turn one over and show that many counters on the workmat. Repeat.

 Discuss It How do you know you have the correct number of counters?

Connect It

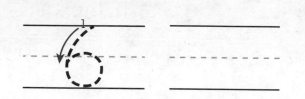

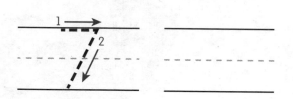

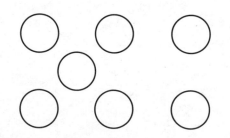 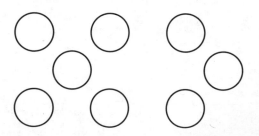

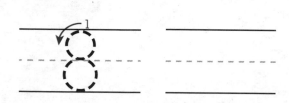

Ask children to find the group that shows 6, 7, or 8. Have children read the number at the beginning of each problem. Then have them trace and write the numeral. Have children color the group with the correct number of objects.

 How did you decide which group of circles to color? What are different ways you could count the group of 8 circles?

Practice Counting and Writing to 10

Example

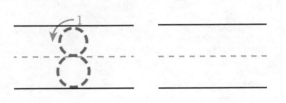

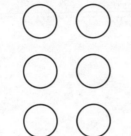

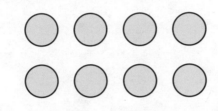

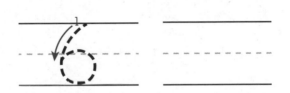

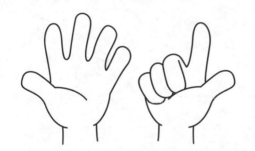

Have children practice writing 6, 7, and 8 and counting 6, 7, and 8 objects.
Ask children to trace and then write the numeral at the beginning of each problem. Then have children color the group with that number of objects.

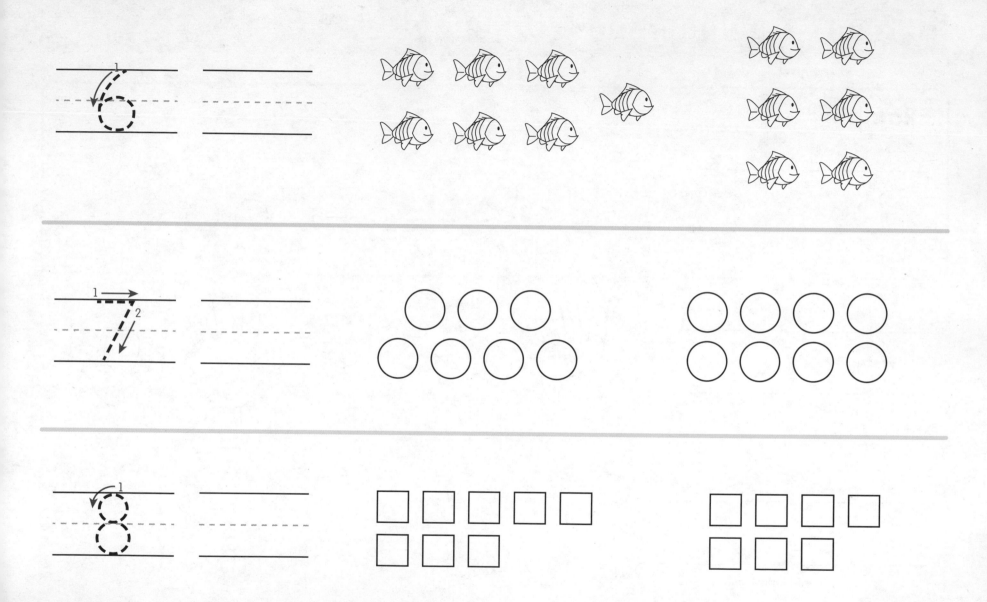

Have children practice writing 6, 7, and 8 and counting 6, 7, and 8 objects.
Ask children to trace and then write the numeral at the beginning of each
problem. Then have children color the group with that number of objects.

Refine Counting and Writing to 10

Apply It

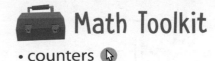

Math Toolkit

• counters

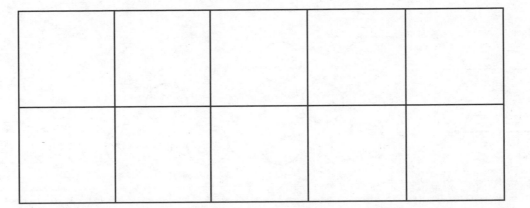

Have children count 9 or 10 counters. Give pairs of children a cup of 20 counters. Have one child count out 9 counters and the second child check by placing the counters on the 10-frame. Children then switch roles. Repeat with counting out 10 counters.

 How does the 10-frame help you check that you have counted the correct number?

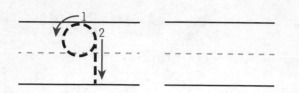

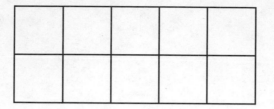

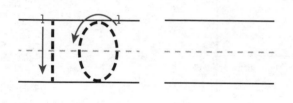

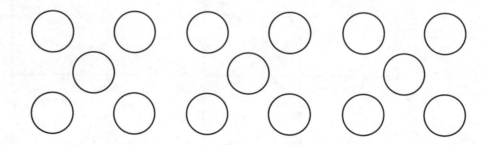

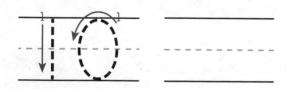

Ask children to trace and write the numerals 9 and 10 and then color 9 or 10 objects.
Note that they may choose to color any 9 or 10 of the objects in the groups. In the last
problem, have children trace and write 10 and then draw 10 shapes or objects.

 Work with a partner. How did your partner
draw 10? How can you check that you both
drew 10 objects correctly?

Practice Counting and Writing to 10

Example

Have children practice writing 9 and 10 and counting out 9 or 10 objects.
Ask children to trace and write the numeral 9 or 10. Then have children color that number of objects.

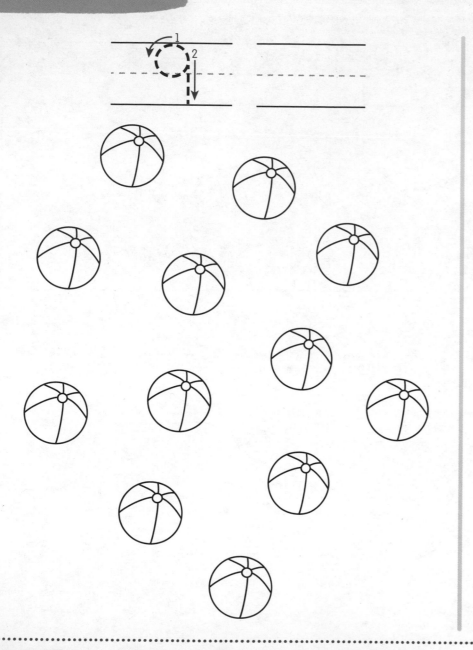

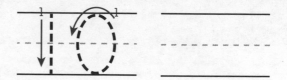

Have children trace and write the numerals 9 and 10, count and color 9 objects, and then draw 10 objects. On the left, have children trace and write the numeral 9 and then color 9 objects. On the right, ask children to trace and write the numeral 10 and then draw a picture to show 10 objects.

Refine Counting and Writing to 10

Apply It

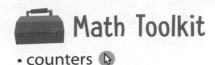

Math Toolkit
• counters

1 2 3 4 5 6 7 8 9 10

Have children find a missing number from the 1 to 10 sequence. Have children work in pairs. One child covers one of the numbers. The other child figures out which number is covered and shows it with counters on the 10-frame.

Discuss It How did you find the missing number?

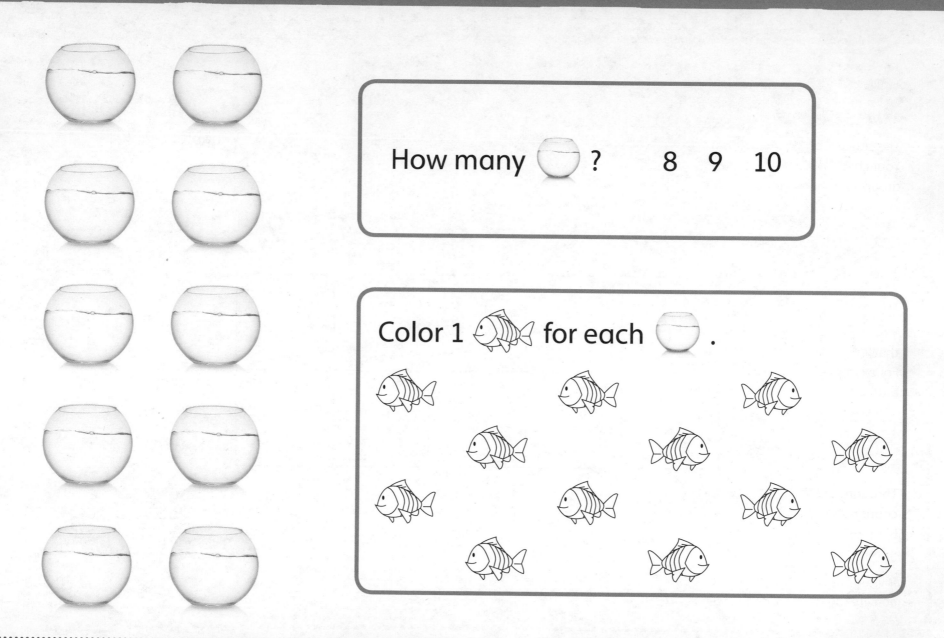

How many ⬭ ?   8   9   10

Color 1 🐟 for each ⬭ .

Have children count the fishbowls and circle the number that tells how many and then color 1 fish for each bowl. Allow children to find their own strategies to figure out how many fish and which ones to color.

Discuss It Work with a partner. Did you color the same fish as your partner? How many fish do not have a bowl?

Understand 1 More

Dear Family,

This week your child is exploring 1 more.

The concept of 1 more builds on the understanding and skill of counting numbers. Your child will begin by counting a group of objects, add 1 more object to the group, and then count again to find the new total.

| 1 | 2 | 3 | 4 | 5 |

Your child will then progress to number paths, where he or she will see that 1 more than a number is the next number in the counting sequence. For example, to find 1 more than 6, he or she can find 6 on the number path and then circle the next number:

| 1 | 2 | 3 | 4 | 5 | 6 | (7) | 8 | 9 | 10 |

Throughout this lesson, your child is prompted to make the connection between the counting sequence and the understanding that the next number in the counting sequence is 1 more than the previous number. This concept will give a deeper understanding into the number system we use.

Invite your child to share what he or she knows about finding 1 more by doing the following activity together.

Activity Finding 1 More

Do this activity with your child to understand 1 more.

Materials paper, pencil, crayons, paper clip, penny, dime

Tell your child that you are going to play a game where you will be racing to the finish.

- Draw a number path from 1 to 10 in the style of a board game, and draw a spinner with 0, 0, 1, and 1, as shown.

- Place the penny and the dime on the number 1. Have your child choose which coin will be his or her game piece (the other will be yours).

- Take turns to spin the spinner and move the coin forward when a 1 is spun.

- When your child spins a 1, have him or her say which number the coin is on and then the number the coin will move to.

- Have your child say which number your coin will move to when you spin a 1.

- The first person to reach the finish (the number 10) wins.

Explore 1 More

Try It

Learning Target

- Understand that each successive number name refers to a quantity that is one larger.

SMP 1, 2, 3, 4, 5, 6, 7, 8

🧰 **Math Toolkit**

- counters

1 2 3 4 5 6 7 8 9 10

Have children explore 1 more than a number by working through the counting numbers from 1 to 10. Give children 10 counters. Have them start at 1 and place a counter on each number in order. Have children say the number as they place the counter. Check that children say the numbers in the correct order, without skipping any. Ask: *How many counters are you putting down each time as you count?*

Lesson 7 Understand 1 More   **127**

Connect It

_____
- - - - - - - -
_____

_____
- - - - - - - -
_____

_____
- - - - - - - -
_____

Have children add 1 more and count to find the total. Give children 7 counters. Have children place the counters on the red counter pictures, counting as they go. Then have them place 1 more and trace around it. Have children count the total number of counters and write the number.

Prepare for Finding 1 More

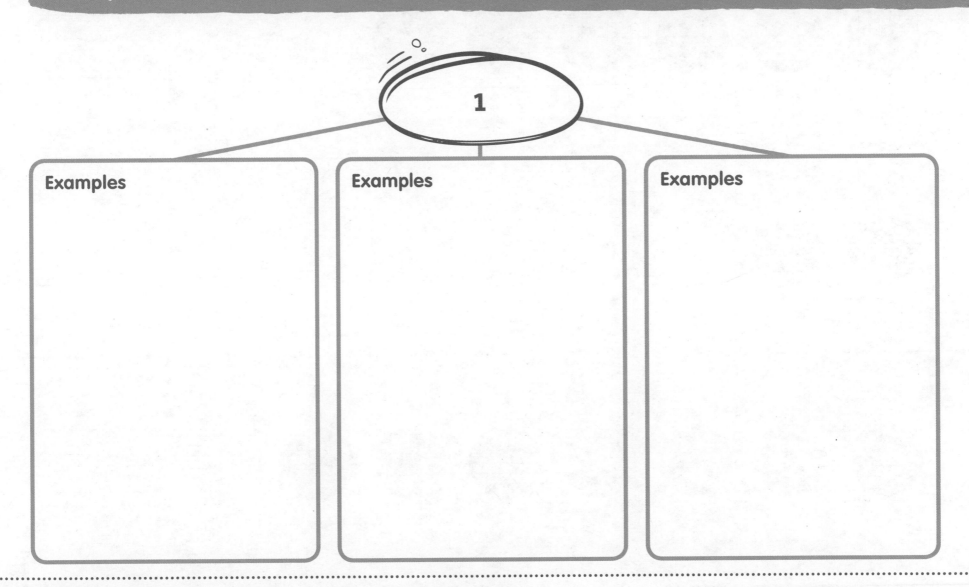

	1	
Examples	**Examples**	**Examples**

Have children show the meaning of 1. Have children fill in each of the boxes to show the meaning of 1. Tell children that they can use words, numbers, and pictures. Encourage them to show as many ideas as they can.

Have children add 1 more and count to find the total. Give children 9 small objects. Have children place the objects on the red counter pictures, counting as they go. Then have them place 1 more and trace around it. Have children count the total number of objects and write the number.

Develop Understanding of 1 More

Model It

How can you show 1 more than 5?

Ask children to draw a picture that could show 1 more than 5. For example, children might draw a group of 5 books and then 1 more book separated from the group. Have children share and discuss their drawings, using the term *1 more*.

Discuss It Tell a story involving your drawing and *1 more*.

Connect It

1 More

_____ | _____

- - - - - | - - - - -

_____ | _____

_____ | _____

- - - - - | - - - - -

_____ | _____

_____ | _____

- - - - - | - - - - -

_____ | _____

Have children find 1 more than a group of objects. Have children count how many are in each group and write the number in the first column. Then ask children to draw 1 more object, count again, and write the number in the next column.

Discuss It Think about the counting numbers. What do you notice about the numbers you have written before and after drawing 1 more?

Think About 1 More

How can you show 1 more than 6?

Ask children to draw a picture that could show 1 more than 6. For example, children might draw a group of 6 pencils and then 1 more pencil separated from the group. Have children share and discuss their drawings, using the term *1 more*.

1 More

Have children find 1 more than a group of objects. Have children count how many are in each group and write the number in the first column.

Then have children draw 1 more object, count again, and write the number in the next column.

Develop Understanding of 1 More

Model It

| 1 | 2 | 3 | 4 | 5 | 6 | 7 | 8 | 9 | 10 |

3

7

6

8

Have children use a number path to find 1 more. Have children find the number 7 and color that space. Have them think about how they can use the number path to find which number is 1 more. Then have them draw a line from the number 7 to the number that is 1 more.

Discuss It How can you use the number path to find the number that is 1 more than the number 3?

Connect It

| 1 | 2 | 3 | 4 | 5 | 6 | 7 | 8 | 9 | 10 |

| 1 | 2 | 3 | 4 | 5 | 6 | 7 | 8 | 9 | 10 |

| 1 | 2 | 3 | 4 | 5 | 6 | 7 | 8 | 9 | 10 |

Encourage children to use number paths to find 1 more than a number. Have children look at the number on the balloon and then, starting at 1 on the number path, color all the way to that number. Have children circle the next number to show what is 1 more.

Discuss It How does coloring the number path show what number is 1 more than a number?

136   **Lesson 7** Understand 1 More

Practice Finding 1 More

Example

2

| 1 | 2 | (3) | 4 | 5 | 6 | 7 | 8 | 9 | 10 |

8

| 1 | 2 | 3 | 4 | 5 | 6 | 7 | 8 | 9 | 10 |

5

| 1 | 2 | 3 | 4 | 5 | 6 | 7 | 8 | 9 | 10 |

Have children use number paths to find 1 more than a number. Have children look at the number on the balloon and then, starting at 1 on the number path, color all the way to that number. Have children circle the next number to show what is 1 more.

 **3**

| 1 | 2 | 3 | 4 | 5 | 6 | 7 | 8 | 9 | 10 |

 **1**

| 1 | 2 | 3 | 4 | 5 | 6 | 7 | 8 | 9 | 10 |

 **7**

7   8   9

Have children use number paths to find 1 more than a number. Have children look at the number on the balloon and then, starting at 1 on the number path, color all the way to that number. Have children circle the next number to show what is 1 more. For the last problem, have children circle the number that is 1 more.

138   **Lesson 7** Understand 1 More

Refine Ideas About 1 More

Apply It

🧰 Math Toolkit
• counters
• number paths

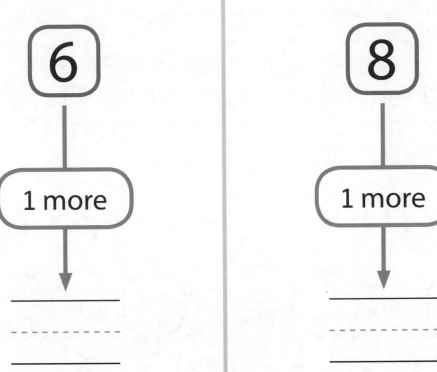

6	8	3
↓	↓	↓
1 more	1 more	1 more
↓	↓	↓
_____	_____	_____

Have children find 1 more than a number. Allow children to use counters on a number path if they need it to find the number that is 1 more than the given number. Have children write the number that is 1 more.

Discuss It How do counting numbers help you find 1 more than a number?

Connect It

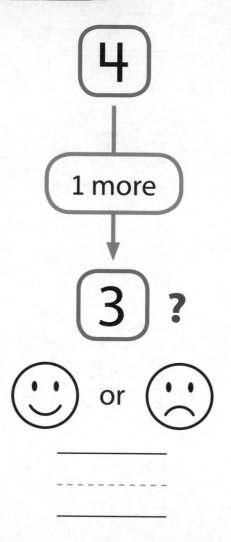

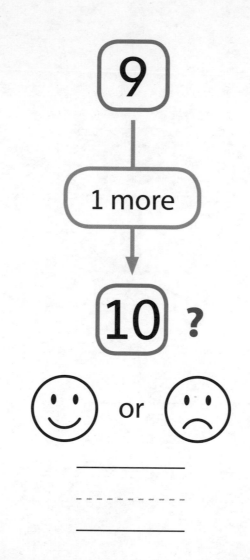

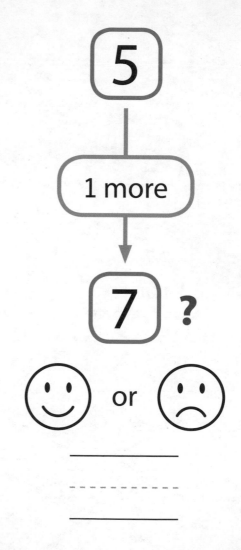

Ask children to check whether each arrow points to the number that is 1 more. Have them color the happy face if the number is correct or the sad face if it is not. Then have children write the correct number that is 1 more.

Discuss It What did you do to check whether the numbers were correct?

Compare Within 10

Dear Family,

This week your child is learning to compare within 10.

The lesson includes comparing groups of up to 10 objects to find which group has more and which group has fewer. There are many strategies that can be used in comparing. When comparing objects in a picture, you can draw lines between the objects in the two groups or cross out pairs of objects (one from each group) until one group has no more objects to cross out. If comparing actual objects, you may line them up in two rows to see which group has more and which has fewer.

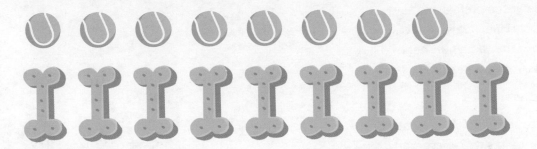

As your child begins to think more abstractly, he or she will start to recognize that 7 is more than 4, no matter what objects are being counted or how they are arranged.

Comparing groups of objects will help prepare your child for solving subtraction problems that involve finding how many more or how many fewer objects are in one group than another.

Invite your child to share what he or she knows about comparing within 10 by doing the following activity together.

Activity Comparing Within 10

Do this activity with your child to explore comparing within 10.

Materials 20 small objects of 2 different kinds (such as 10 crackers and 10 pretzels, or 10 buttons and 10 paper clips), 2 bowls

- Place 10 objects of one kind in a bowl for your child. Place 10 objects of another kind in a bowl for yourself.

- You and your child each take a handful of objects and place them on the table. Your child compares the groups of objects using any strategy he or she prefers and says which group has more. For example, if there are 8 crackers and 3 pretzels, your child should say: *8 is more than 3.* (Sometimes the groups will have the same number of objects. If that is the case, add objects to or remove objects from your group.)

- Return the objects to the bowls and repeat the activity several times.

- Now tell your child you are going to compare the groups to see which has fewer. For example, if there are 8 crackers and 3 pretzels, your child should say: *3 is less than 8.*

In addition to doing the above activity, encourage your child to compare numbers of objects in his or her daily life. For example, ask your child to compare numbers of buttons and pockets, cups and plates, or swings and slides.

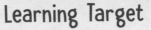
Explore Comparing Within 10

Learning Target

- Compare two numbers between 1 and 10 presented as written numerals.

SMP 1, 2, 3, 4, 5, 6, 8

 Math Toolkit

- counters
- crayons

Children compare groups of 6 and 7 crayons and discuss how to identify the group that has more. Invite two children to the front of the class and give one child 6 crayons and the other 7 crayons. Ask: *Which child* *has more crayons? How do you know?* Then have children use counters to model the problem and discuss how they can compare the number of counters without counting.

Lesson 8 Compare Within 10   **143**

Connect It

Children compare groups of counters to see which has more. Pair children and give each child a group of 5, 6, or 7 counters. Then ask children to compare the counters to find out which child has more or if they have the same number of counters. Ask pairs to explain how they determined who has more. Then display 5 crayons in one hand and 7 crayons in the other. Ask: *Which hand has more crayons? How do you know?*

Prepare for Comparing Within 10

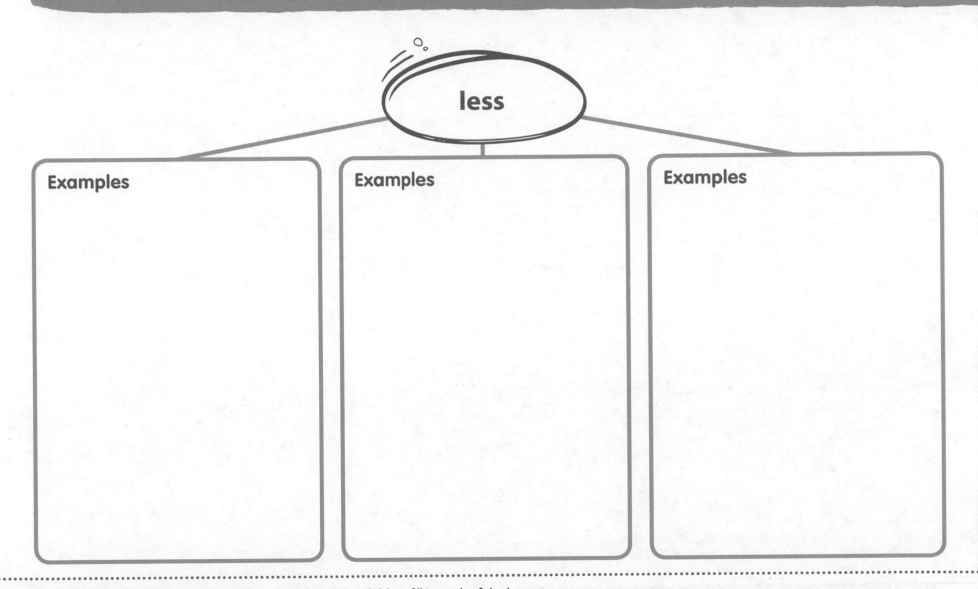

less

Examples

Examples

Examples

Have children show the meaning of the word *less*. Have children fill in each of the boxes to show the meaning of the word *less*. Tell children that they can use words, numbers, and pictures. Encourage them to show as many ideas as they can.

Children compare groups of objects to see which has fewer. Give children some small objects. Have them put 3 objects on one workmat and 2 objects on the other workmat. Then ask children to compare the objects to find out which workmat has fewer. Ask them to explain how they determined which has fewer. Then have them place 3 objects on one workmat and 4 objects on the other workmat. Ask: *Which workmat has fewer objects? How do you know?*

Develop Comparing Within 10

Encourage children to discuss the quantities of items and then compare quantities.
Ask children to make comparison statements using *more, less, fewer,* or *the same as.* Have children draw lines matching each puppy to a collar.

Discuss It Do you think the pet store sells more dog treats than balls? Why or why not?

Connect It

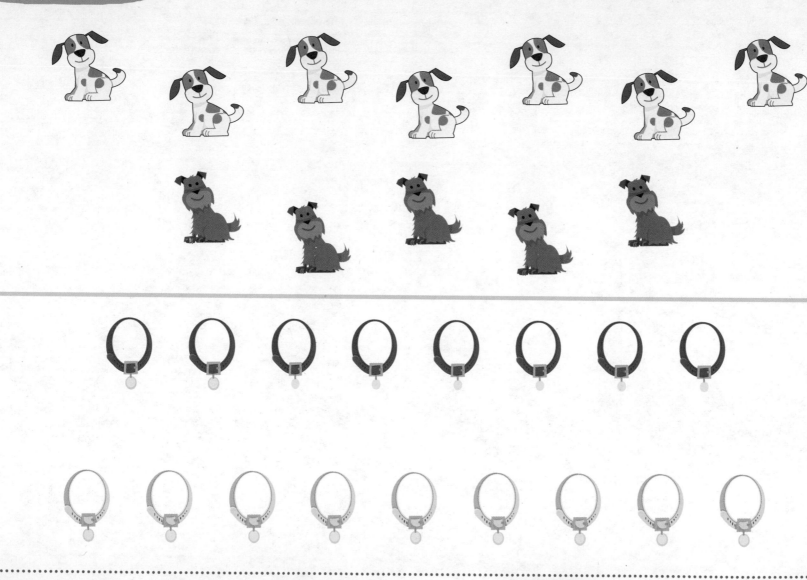

Have children draw lines to match objects and circle the group with more. For each problem, ask children to tell which group has more and explain how they know.

Discuss It How does drawing lines to match objects help you know which group has more?

Practice Comparing Within 10

Have children count and color the 8 dogs. Have children color green a group that has fewer than 8. Have them color brown a group that has more than 8. Then have children color the rest of the picture.

Have children draw lines to match objects and circle the group with fewer.
For each problem, ask children to tell which group has fewer and explain how
they know.

Develop Comparing Within 10

 Try It

 Math Toolkit

• counters

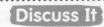

Have children compare groups of counters to see which has more. Tell children how many counters to put in each bowl. Use 5 to 10 counters in each bowl. Then ask them to compare the counters to find out which bowl has more and which bowl has fewer.

Discuss It Which bowl would have more if there were 9 counters in each bowl?

Connect It

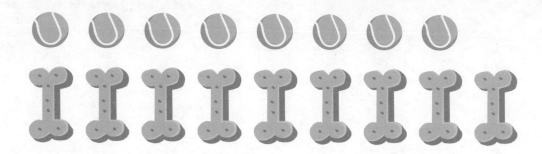

_____

- - - - - - - - - **or** - - - - - - - - -

_____

_____

- - - - - - - - - **or** - - - - - - - - -

_____

_____

- - - - - - - - - **or** - - - - - - - - -

_____

Have children compare the quantities shown in the pictures. Have children write how many are in each group, read each number, and then circle the number that is greater. For each problem, discuss different ways to decide which group has more.

Discuss It Work with a partner. Look at the green and pink dots. Is there one pink dot for every green dot? How can you be sure?

Name: _____

Practice Comparing Within 10

Example

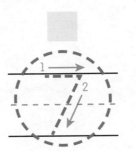 or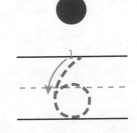

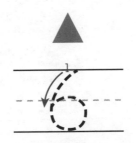 or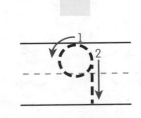

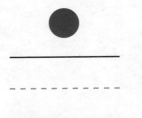 or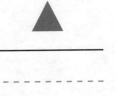

In each problem, have children compare the numbers of objects.
Have children write how many are in each group and then circle the number that is greater.

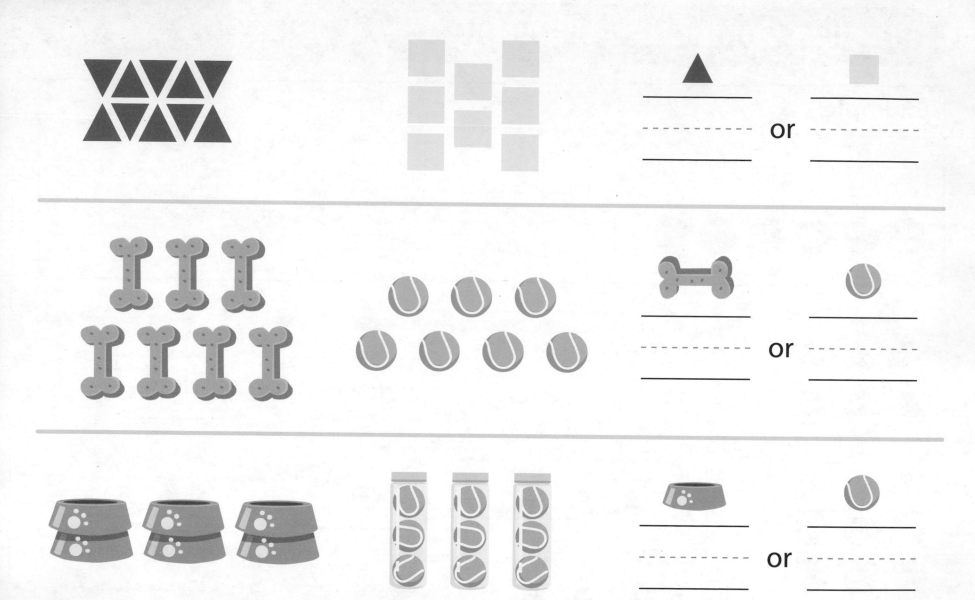

In each problem, have children compare the numbers of objects. Have children write how many are in each group and then circle the number that is less. If the groups have the same number, have children circle both numbers.

Refine Comparing Within 10

Apply It

Which is less?

Math Toolkit
- counters
- 10-frames

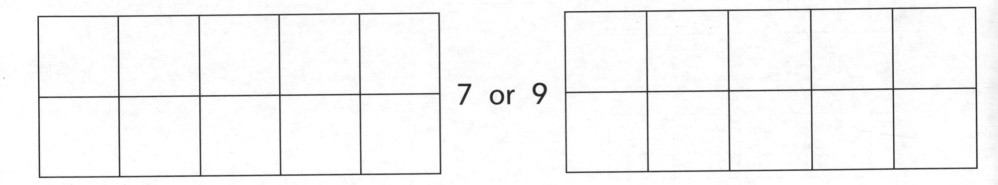

7 or 9

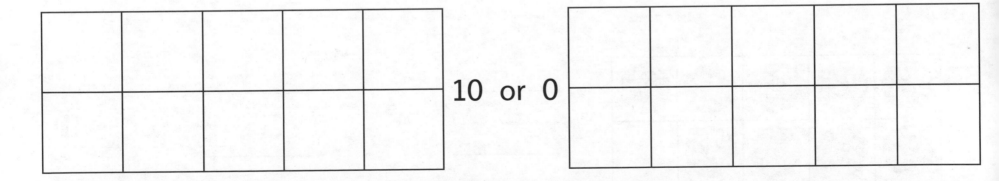

10 or 0

Ask children to compare numbers. First have them compare numbers and tell which is less. Have children represent each number with counters to check their comparisons. For each problem, have them circle the number that is less.

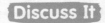 **Discuss It** How did using counters on the 10-frames help you check your comparisons?

How many?

Which is less?

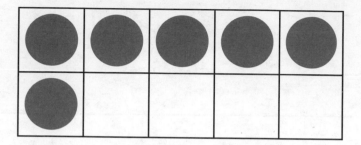

_____
\- \- \- \- \- \- \-
_____

_____
\- \- \- \- \- \- \-
_____   or   5

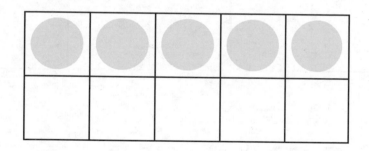

_____
\- \- \- \- \- \- \-
_____

_____
\- \- \- \- \- \- \-
_____   or   7

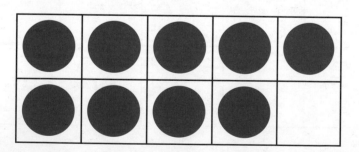

_____
\- \- \- \- \- \- \-
_____

_____
\- \- \- \- \- \- \-
_____   or   10

Have children compare the number of counters in a 10-frame with a given number and tell which is less. Have them count and write the number of counters in the 10-frame, compare that number with the number shown in black, and circle the number that is less.

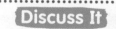 **Discuss It** Look at all the counters. Which group of counters shows the number closest to 10? How do you know?

Name: _____

Practice Comparing Within 10

Example

How many?

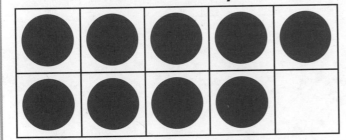

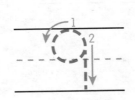

Which is greater?

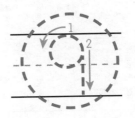   or   7

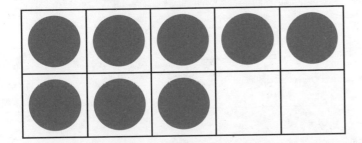

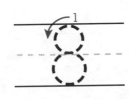

_____

- - - - - - - - - -

   or   6

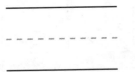

_____

- - - - - - - - - -
_____

   or   10

Have children compare the number of counters in a 10-frame with a given number and tell which is greater. Have children count and write the number of counters in the 10-frame. Ask them to compare that number with the number shown on the right. Have them circle the number that is greater.

How many?

Which is less?

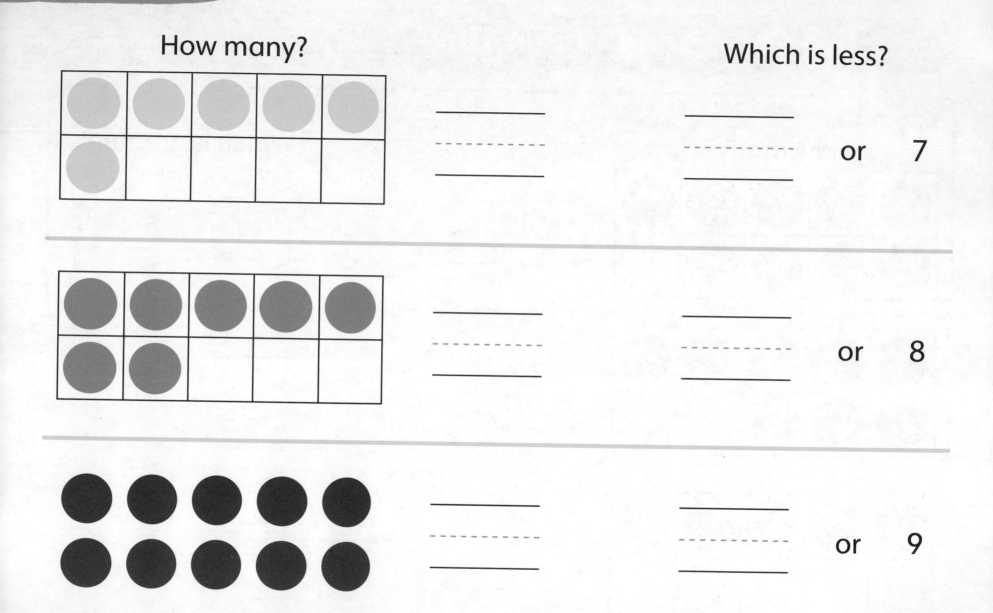

_____   _____

- - - - - -   - - - - - -   or   7

_____   _____

_____   _____

- - - - - -   - - - - - -   or   8

_____   _____

_____   _____

- - - - - -   - - - - - -   or   9

_____   _____

Ask children to compare a number of counters with a given number and tell which is less. Have children count and write the number of counters. Ask them to compare that number with the number shown on the right. Have them circle the number that is less.

Refine Comparing Within 10

Apply It

 Math Toolkit
- counters
- number cubes (labeled 5–10)
- 10-frames

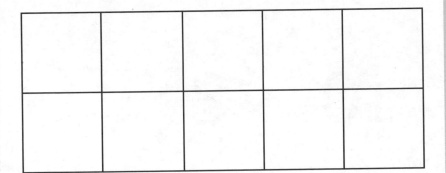 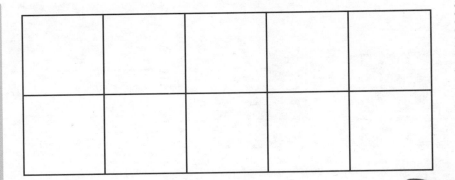

Have children tell which number is greater and which is less. Have partners roll two number cubes (labeled 5–10). Ask them to say which number is greater and which is less and then use counters to build the numbers on the 10-frames to check. Repeat.

Discuss It How can you tell which number is greater before you check your answer with counters?

Greater

6	8	____
9	7	____
10	6	____

Less

6	9	____
10	8	____
7	8	____

Have children determine which number is greater and which is less. For each pair of numbers in the first column, ask children to write the number that is greater. In the second column, ask them to write the number that is less.

Discuss It Check your work. How can you be sure which number is greater? How can you be sure which number is less?

Sort and Count Objects

Dear Family,

This week your child is learning to sort objects.

Actual objects and pictures of objects can be **sorted** by attributes such as color, shape, size, and weight. After sorting objects into different categories, your child will count how many are in each group and compare the groups using language such as *same, equal, more than, fewer than*, and *less than*.

For example, the fish below can be sorted into the following categories: big and small, striped and solid, swimming left and swimming right. Also, there are more solid fish than striped fish, and there are fewer big fish, than small fish.

Sorting objects into groups, as well as counting and comparing the numbers of objects in each group, will help your child prepare to work with charts and graphs in later grades.

Invite your child to share what he or she knows about sorting objects by doing the following activity together.

Activity | Sorting Objects

Do this activity with your child to practice sorting and counting objects.

Materials 8 to 10 objects that can be sorted by size, color, shape, and/or other attributes (such as buttons, beads, blocks, coins, or dried beans)

- Give your child 8 to 10 objects of at least two different shapes, colors, and/or sizes. They should be able to be sorted two different ways, such as by size and then by color.

- Ask your child to sort some or all of the objects into two groups. If needed, you can suggest sorting by shape, color, or size. Encourage your child to tell you about the groups. Ask him or her how many are in each group and which group has more or fewer.

- Then ask your child to sort some or all of the objects into two groups in a different way. For example, if the objects are first sorted by color, they can then be sorted by size. Discuss what the new groups look like.

- For an additional challenge, add objects of a different shape, color, or size and ask your child to sort the objects into three groups.

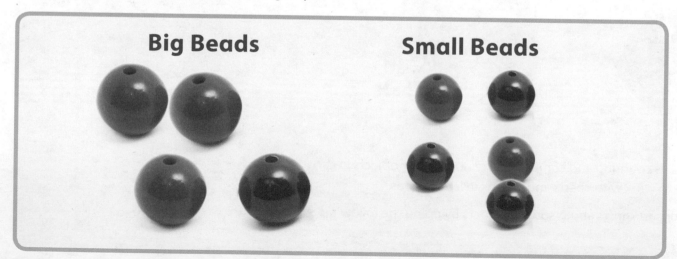

Big Beads

Small Beads

Explore Sorting and Counting Objects

Learning Target

- Classify objects into given categories; count the numbers of objects in each category and sort the categories by count.

SMP 1, 2, 3, 4, 5, 6, 7

Children sort books, then count and compare the number in each group. Have children sort books into groups by size and count to find the total in each group. Write the totals on the board and have children write the numbers. As a class, compare the numbers using language such as *more than, fewer than, the same as,* and *equal.* Repeat, having the class sort the books another way.

Connect It

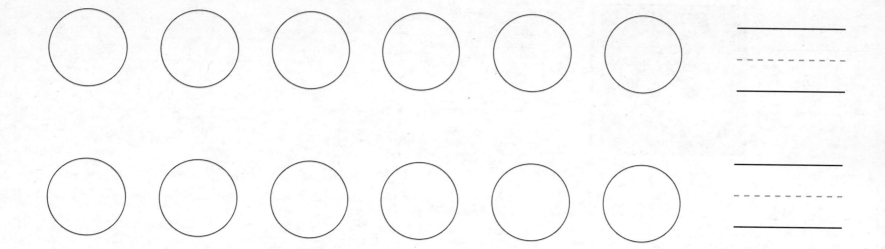

Have children determine the categories used to sort. Invite 5 children with short names and 6 with long names to the front. Have children identify the categories used to sort and find the total in each group. Children color the top row of circles to show the number in the short names group and the bottom row to show the number in the long names group. Then children write the totals and compare the numbers.

Prepare for Sorting and Counting Objects

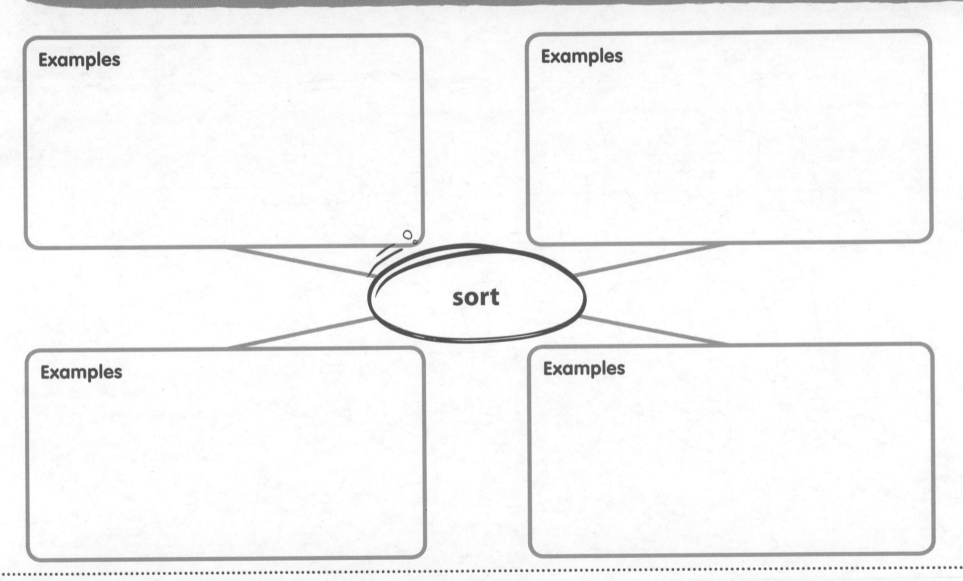

Examples

Examples

sort

Examples

Examples

Have children show the meaning of the word *sort*. Have children fill in each of the boxes to show the meaning of the word *sort*. Tell children that they can use words, numbers, and pictures. Encourage them to show as many ideas as they can.

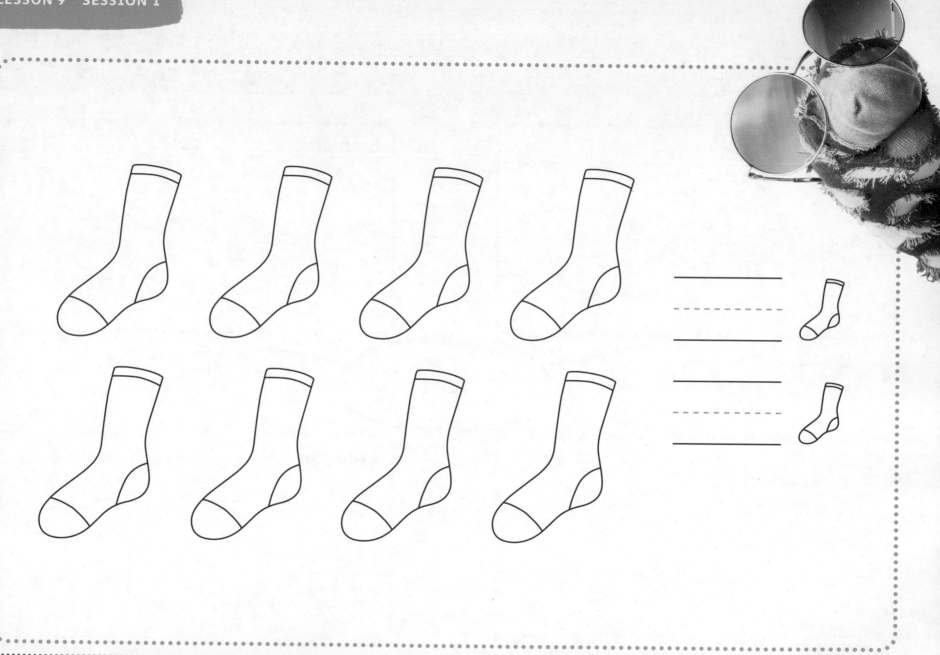

Have children sort a group of socks. Give children 8 socks, some red and some blue (or a different pair of colors). Have children sort the socks by color. Then have children color one sock red for every red sock and one sock blue for every blue sock (or the colors of the socks they have). Then have children color one small sock red and one blue, count how many of each they have colored, and then write each total and compare the numbers.

Develop Sorting and Counting Objects

Have children sort objects based on color, size, or feature. Ask probing questions, such as: *How many bubbles are big? How many are small?* Have children circle the striped fish and then count the number of striped and not-striped fish.

Discuss It Describe two different ways you could sort the rocks.

Math Toolkit
• counters

Have children sort by size, color, or feature. Have children describe how they could sort the fish. Ask: *How many big fish are there? How many small fish?* Point to the plant. Ask: *How many fish are swimming toward the plant?* Have children circle them and count.

Discuss It How do you find out which group has more? What other ways can you sort them? How would you describe the whole group?

Practice Sorting and Counting Objects

Have children color the striped fish red and the rest of the fish yellow.
Then have children color the big rocks one color and the small rocks a
different color. Have children color the rest of the picture.

Have children sort objects based on feature. Discuss with children how the objects shown are similar and different. Prompt children to see that some objects can be eaten while others cannot. Have children color all the objects that can be eaten. Then have children count the objects they colored and compare that number to the number of objects that are not colored.

Develop Sorting and Counting Objects

Try It

Math Toolkit

• connecting cubes

Have children sort pictures of objects into two groups. Have children choose a way to sort and then circle the objects that fit their rule. Count and compare the numbers in each group. Children explain their rule to a partner or swap papers and try to guess the rule.

Discuss It How can you tell which group has fewer objects? How can using cubes help you sort the groups and find which group has more?

Connect It

Ask children to name one object that does not belong with the others. Explain that there is more than one correct answer. Have children cross out one object they see as different. Have children share their answers and the reasons for each.

Discuss It How did you decide which object to cross out?

172 **Lesson 9** Sort and Count Objects

Practice Sorting and Counting Objects

Example

Ask children to name one object that does not belong with the others.
Explain that there may be more than one correct answer. Have children cross

out one object they see as different. Then have children share the reasons for
crossing out each object.

Ask children to name one object that does not belong with the others.
Explain that there may be more than one correct answer. Have children cross out one object they see as different. Then have children share the reasons for crossing out each object.

Refine Sorting and Counting Objects

Apply It

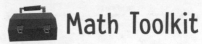 **Math Toolkit**

- attribute blocks
- buttons
- crayons

Have children sort and count objects and compare groups. Give children 10 objects, such as buttons or attribute blocks. Have children sort the objects into two groups, for example, by size or by color. Ask children to count each group and say which has fewer.

 How can you tell how many are in each group? How can you tell which group has fewer? What other ways can the objects be sorted?

Lesson 9 Sort and Count Objects   **175**

Ask children to sort the objects. Prompt children to realize that the two given groups are big objects and small objects. Have children circle the objects at the bottom of the page with a blue or green crayon to show which group they belong to.

Discuss It What are some other objects that could go in the blue box? How did you decide?

Practice Sorting and Counting Objects

Example

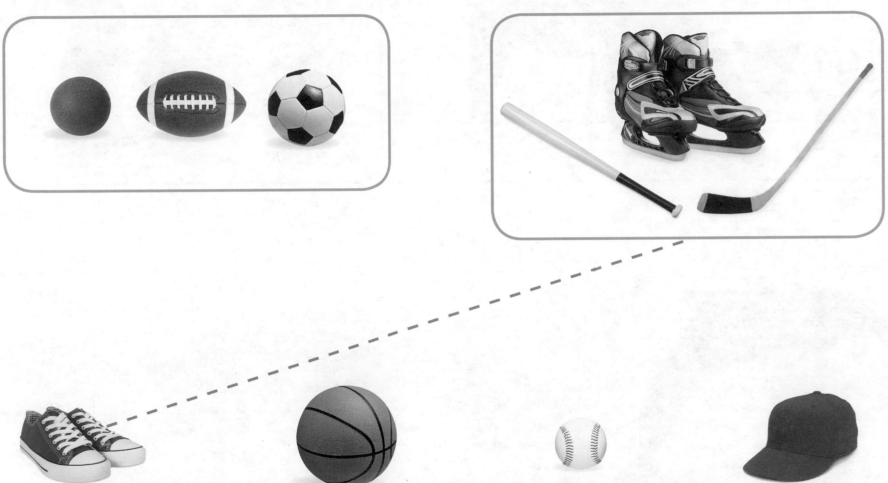

Ask children to sort the objects. Prompt children to realize that the two given groups are balls and other sports items. Have children draw a line from each object at the bottom of the page to the group to which it belongs.

Have children sort the animals. Prompt children to realize that the two given groups are big animals and small animals. Have children draw a line from each animal at the bottom of the page to the group to which it belongs.

Refine Sorting and Counting Objects

Apply It

 **Math Toolkit**
• attribute blocks
• buttons

Have children sort and count objects and then compare groups. Give children 10–15 objects, such as attribute blocks or buttons, and have them sort into three groups by color, size, shape, or other feature. Have children write the number of objects in each group.

Discuss It Which group has more? Which group has fewer? What is another way you could sort these objects?

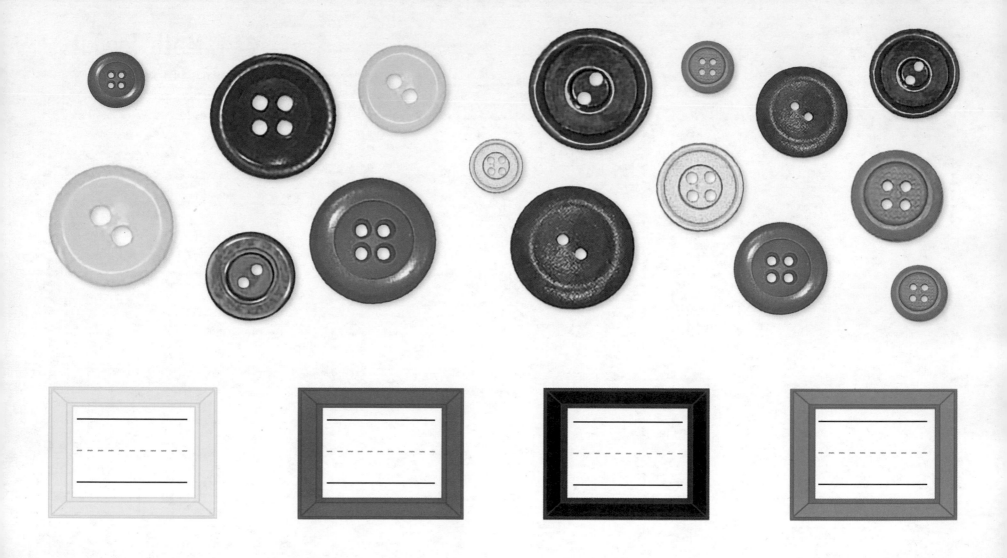

Have children sort the buttons by color. Have children count the number of buttons of each color and write the number in the box of the same color. Have children compare the number of buttons in the yellow group with the number in each of the other groups.

Discuss It Which groups have more? Which groups have fewer? What is another way you could sort these buttons?

Make 10

Dear Family,

This week your child is learning to find the numbers that make 10.

This lesson uses pictures, counters, and 10-frames to find the different combinations of numbers that make 10.

Using a 10-frame helps to visualize 10 as a quantity, as well as visualize the numbers that make 10. For example, by filling a 10-frame in different ways, you can see that 10 is made up of 4 and 6, 7 and 3, and other number pairs. The structure of a 10-frame, which has 2 rows of 5, can also help your child recognize that 10 is made up of 2 groups of 5. Knowing all the ways to make 10 will allow your child to use multiple strategies to add and subtract.

4 and 6

7 and 3

Ways to Make 10	
1 and 9	9 and 1
2 and 8	8 and 2
3 and 7	7 and 3
4 and 6	6 and 4
5 and 5	

Invite your child to share what he or she knows about making 10 by doing the following activity together.

Activity   Making 10

Do this activity with your child to practice making 10.

Materials egg carton (optional), 18 small objects of two different colors or types to place in the egg carton (such as buttons in two different colors, small blocks in two different colors, or dried beans and pasta shapes)

- Cut off two cups at one end of the egg carton. Now that the egg carton has 2 rows of 5 cups, have your child use it like a 10-frame to do the following activity. Instead of using an egg carton, you can draw a 10-frame for your child to use.

- Put some objects of one color in the egg carton, placing them in the top row first and working from left to right.

- Have your child finish filling the egg carton with objects of a different color. Your child should say how the objects in the egg carton show a way to make 10, such as: *4 and 6 make 10.* Repeat until you have found 5 different ways to make 10.

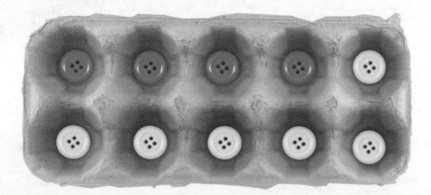

Explore Making 10

Try It

10

 Math Toolkit

- connecting cubes ⬤

Have children explore different ways to make 10. Pose the problem: *How many ways can you make a group of 10 children with some number of children holding a paper of one color and some number of children holding a paper of* *another color?* Invite different groups of 10 children to the front of the room to model combinations of 10. Have children say how each combination is made and then model the combination with connecting cubes.

Connect It

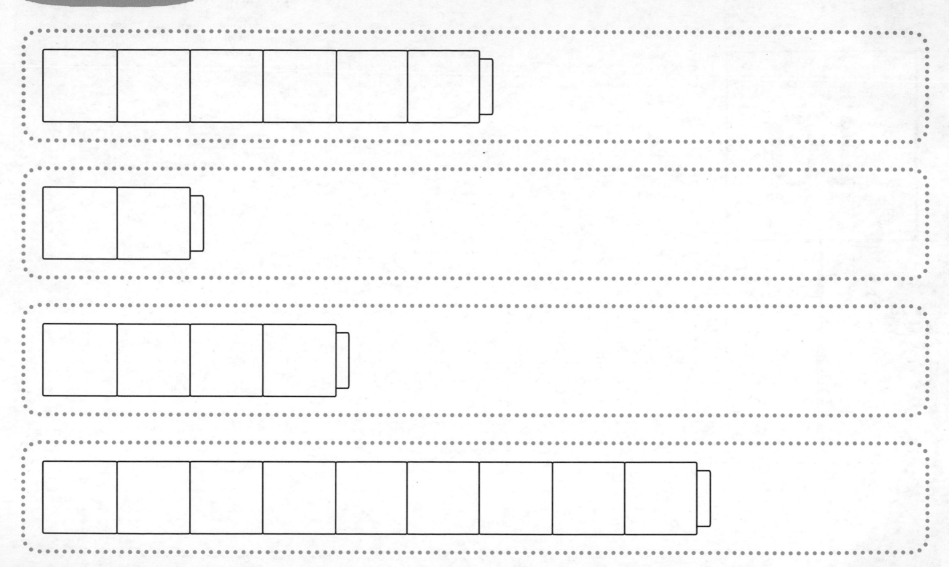

Have children make combinations of 10 starting from a given number.
Display a train of 6 cubes. Ask: *How many more cubes do I need to have 10?*

Have children model the problem using connecting cubes. Repeat, starting with 2, 4, and 9 cubes.

Prepare for Making 10

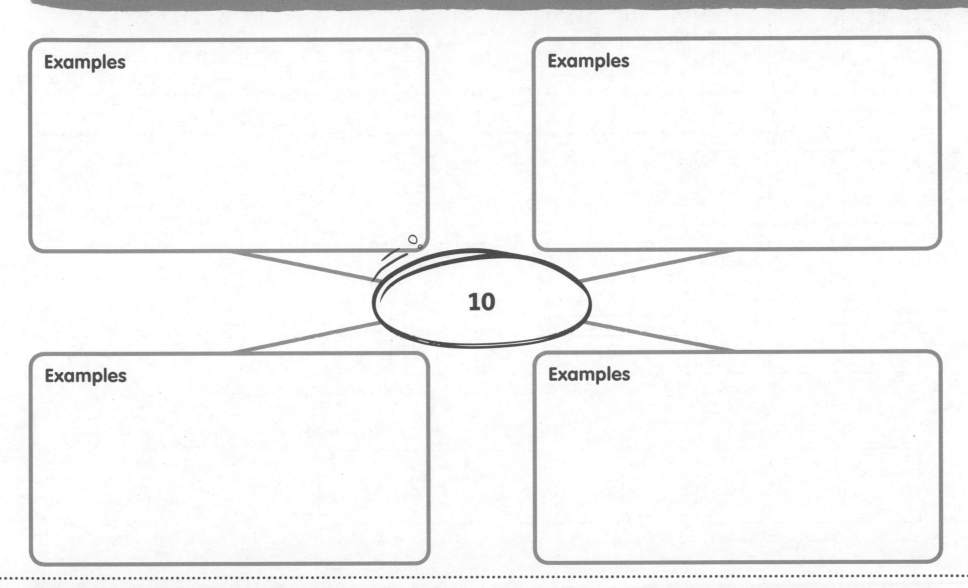

Examples

Examples

10

Examples

Examples

Have children show the meaning of 10. Have children fill in each of the boxes to show the meaning of 10. Tell children that they can use words, numbers, and pictures. Encourage them to show as many ideas as they can.

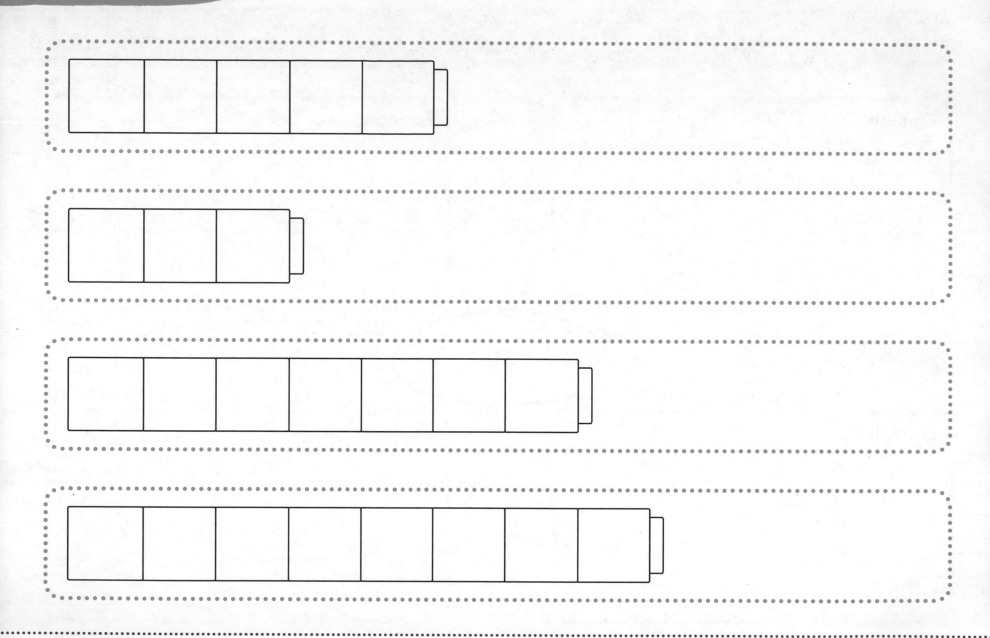

Have children make combinations of 10 starting from a given number.
Point out the train of 5 cubes. Ask: *How many more cubes do I need to have 10?*

Have children use objects to model the problem. Repeat, starting with 3, 7, and 8 cubes.

Develop Making 10

Encourage children to describe the number of each type of ball as the total of two numbers. Ask children to name the number pairs shown for each group of balls. Say: *Jake needs 10 red balls*. Have children draw more red balls to make 10.

Discuss It How are the number of baseball bats and the number of baseballs the same? How are they different?

Connect It

5 and 5

9 and 1

2 and 8

Have children draw lines to match each group of 10 to the number pair that describes the group. Then have children describe the group of 10, such as: *This group of 10 is made of 9 basketballs and 1 soccer ball.*

Discuss It Can you make 10 if you have 0 in one group? Can you make 10 with two groups that each have the same amount?

188   **Lesson 10** Make 10

Practice Making 10

Have children use two colors to color a group of 10. Then have children use two colors to color another group of 10, this time showing a different number pair. Have children color the rest of the page.

8 and 2

7 and 3

4 and 6

Have children draw lines to match each group of 10 to the number pair that describes the group. Then have children describe the group of 10.

For example, children might say: *This group of 10 is made of 7 cats and 3 dogs.*

Develop Making 10

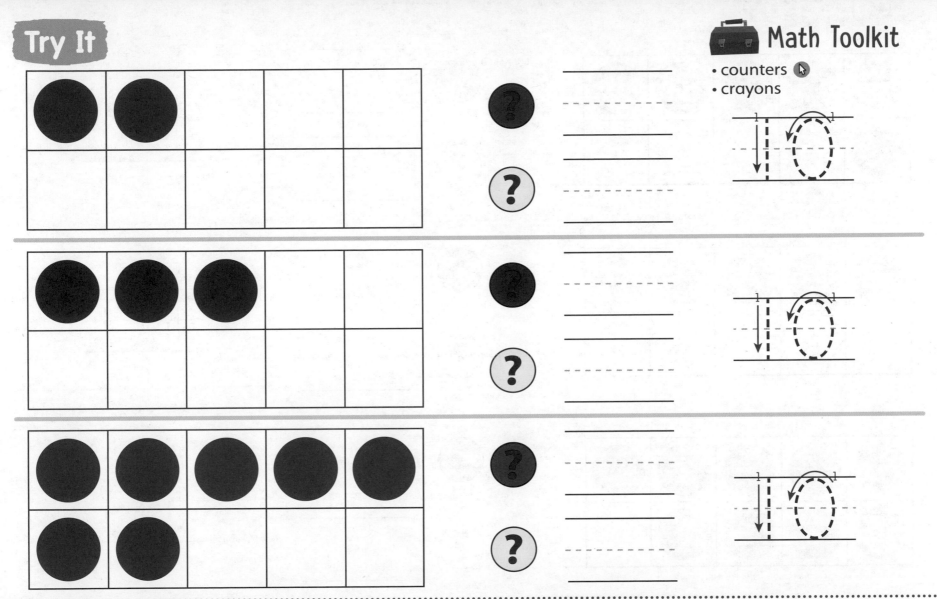

Try It

Math Toolkit
- counters
- crayons

Have children make 10 using counters. Give children 10 yellow counters and have them place the correct number of counters in the remaining spaces on the 10-frame to make 10. Children count, write how many of each color counter make 10, and trace the numeral 10.

Discuss It How do you know how many counters are needed to make 10? How does the 10-frame help you make 10?

Lesson 10 Make 10   **191**

Connect It

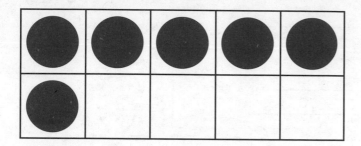

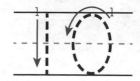

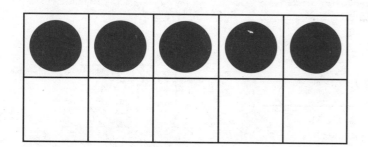

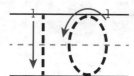

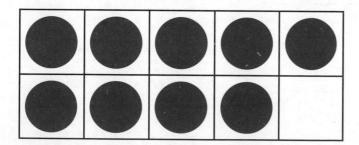

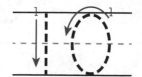

Ask children to draw yellow counters to finish each picture so that it shows 10. Then have children count and write how many counters there are of each color and trace the numeral 10.

Discuss It If you had 6 yellow counters, how many red counters would there be? How do you know?

Practice Making 10

Example

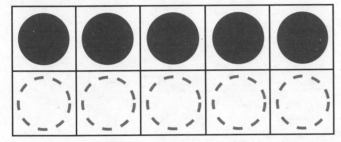

 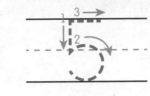 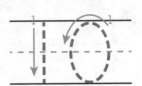

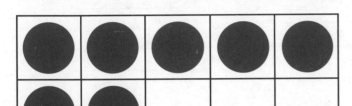

 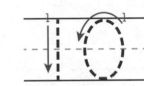

 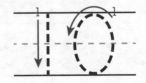

Ask children to draw counters to finish each picture so that it shows 10.
Have children write the number of red counters and the number of counters
that they drew. Finally, have children trace the numeral 10 to show the total.

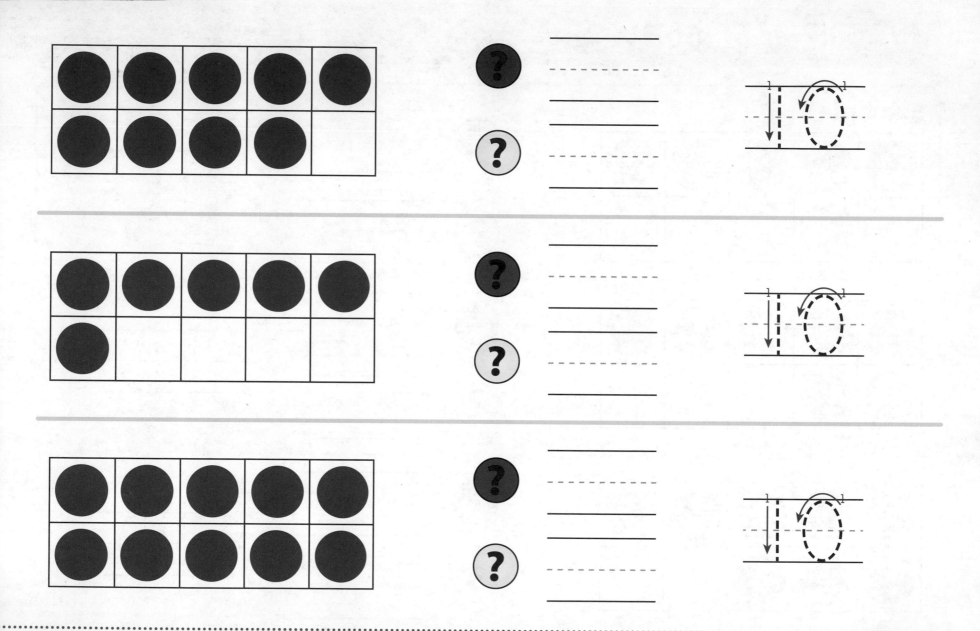

Ask children to draw counters, if needed, to finish each picture so that it shows 10. Have children write the number of red counters shown and the number of counters that they drew. Finally, have children trace the numeral 10 to show the total.

Apply It

Math Toolkit
- two-color counters
- cups
- crayons

_____ and _____ _____ and _____

Have children make 10 using counters. Give children 10 two-color counters in a cup. Have them pour out the counters. Have children place the red counters and write the number. Then have them place the yellow counters and write the number. Repeat.

Discuss It Can the pairs of numbers change? If you have 4 red and 6 yellow, another time could you have 4 red and a different number of yellow?

Ask children to draw three different ways to fill the 10-frames with red and then yellow counters to show a total of 10. Have children count the number of each color, write the number pairs, and then write the total.

Discuss It Is there a way to make 10 using the same number of yellow and red counters? Why or why not?

Name: _____

Practice Making 10

Example

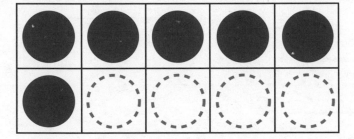 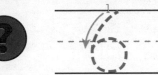 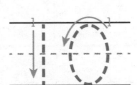 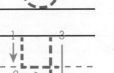

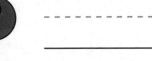  

Ask children to choose three different ways to complete the 10-frames by drawing red and then yellow counters to show a total of 10. For each problem, have children count the number of each color, write the number pair, and then write the total.

Ask children to show three different ways to fill the 10-frames by drawing red and then yellow counters to make a total of 10. For the first two problems, encourage children to show number pairs that are different from those on the previous page. For the last problem, have children show 10 with only one color. For each problem, have children count the number of each color, write the number pair, and then write the total.

Apply It

Math Toolkit
- two-color counters
- crayons

_____
– – –
_____

 ? – – – –

? – – – –

_____
– – –
_____

? – – – –

 ? – – – –

Have children use two-color counters to show two different ways to make 10.
Have children show yellow counters and write the number, repeat with red counters
to make a number pair to 10, and then write the total at the top.

Discuss It How did you find two groups to make 10? How
does using counters help you check that you
have made 10?

_____

- - - - - - - - - - -

_____

_____

- - - - - - - - - - -

_____

? _____

? _____

? _____

? _____

Have children draw two different ways to show 10 and write the number pairs and total.
Say: *Alok has 10 balls. Some are yellow, and the rest are red. How many are yellow? How many are red?* Discuss the different ways that children may have pictured the same number pairs.

 How can you check to see if the ways you made 10 are different?

Make 6, 7, 8, and 9

Dear Family,

This week your child is learning to find number pairs that make 6, 7, 8, and 9.

You can think of numbers as being composed of combinations of other numbers. The number 6 can be made up of 2 and 4, 3 and 3, 5 and 1, or 6 and 0 with the addends in either order. Recognizing number combinations will help your child prepare for adding and subtracting. For example, knowing that 2 and 4 make 6 lays the foundation for solving $2 + 4 = ?$.

In class, your child will show different ways to make 6, 7, 8, and 9 with counters on a 10-frame. Working with a 10-frame will help your child visualize numbers as quantities. It also helps to develop an understanding of how various numbers relate to 5 and 10, which will be important for later work with greater numbers.

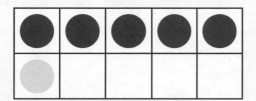

5 and 1 make 6

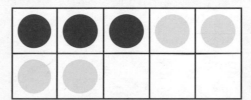

3 and 4 make 7

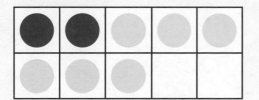

2 and 6 make 8

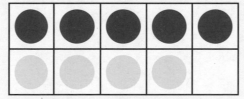

5 and 4 make 9

Invite your child to share what he or she knows about making 6, 7, 8, and 9 by doing the following activity together.

Activity Making 6, 7, 8, and 9

Do this activity with your child to practice making 6, 7, 8, and 9.

Materials 9 pennies (or other coins), 1 cup

- Place 6 pennies in a cup.

- Spill the pennies out onto a table.

- Ask your child to tell you what groups he or she sees. For example, your child may see a group of 4 pennies and a group of 2 pennies based on the position of the pennies on the table. Repeat until you have found several ways to make 6.

- Then repeat the activity with totals of 7, 8, and 9 until your child has found several ways to make each number.

Explore Making 6, 7, 8, and 9

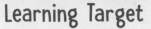

Learning Target

- Decompose numbers less than or equal to 10 into pairs in more than one way, and record each decomposition by a drawing or equation.

SMP 1, 2, 3, 4, 5, 6, 7

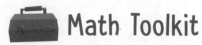 Math Toolkit

- connecting cubes

Children explore different ways to make 6. Say: *6 muffins fit in a box. How can you fill the box with banana muffins and blueberry muffins?* Have children act out combinations of 6 banana and blueberry muffins using yellow and blue paper.

Then have them explore combinations of 6 on the workmat using yellow and blue cubes. Have children use one section for each color.

Connect It

Children explore different ways to make 9. Say: *Let us see how many ways you can make 9.* Invite children to act out combinations of 9 by having some children in a row of 9 stand and some sit. Then have children explore other combinations of 9 with a partner using connecting cubes. Encourage children to count each combination to verify.

Prepare for Making 6, 7, 8, and 9

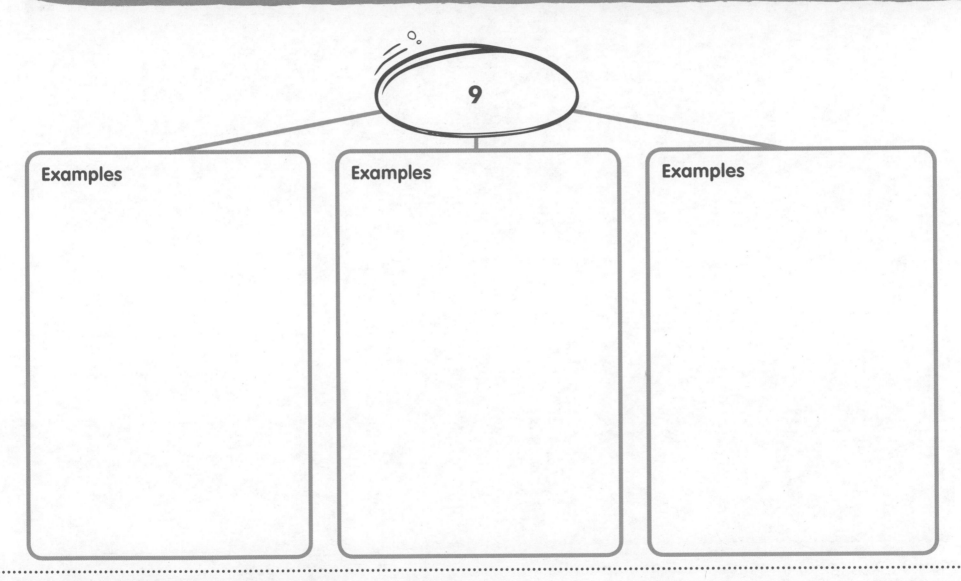

9

| Examples | Examples | Examples |

Have children show the meaning of 9. Have children fill in each of the boxes to show the meaning of 9. Tell children that they can use words, numbers, and pictures. Encourage them to show as many ideas as they can.

Have children explore different ways to make 8. Provide children with coins, dried beans, or pasta. Have them put some of the items in one section of the workmat and the rest of the items in the other section. Encourage children to find different combinations that make 8. Then have children draw one way they made 8.

Develop Making 6, 7, 8, and 9

Have children tell the different numbers that make up the same kind of item, such as 3 green apples and 4 red apples make 7 apples altogether. Ask children to circle two smaller groups that make a larger group.

Discuss It How are the number of fruits in the bowl and the number of flowers the same? How are they different?

Connect It

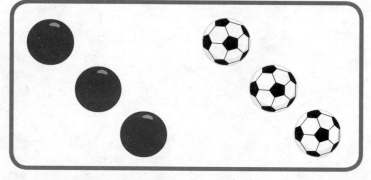

5 and 3

3 and 4

3 and 3

Have children describe the number of objects in each group. Then have children draw lines to match each group of objects to the number pair that describes the group.

Discuss It How do you know which number pair to match to the apples?

Practice Making 6, 7, 8, and 9

Have children use two different colors to color a group of 6, 7, 8, or 9 objects. Ask them to tell you the number pair that they colored. Then repeat the process for another number.

5 and 2

2 and 4

4 and 4

Have children describe the number of objects in each group. Then have children draw lines to match each group of objects to the number pair that describes the group.

210   **Lesson 11**   Make 6, 7, 8, and 9

Develop Making 6, 7, 8, and 9

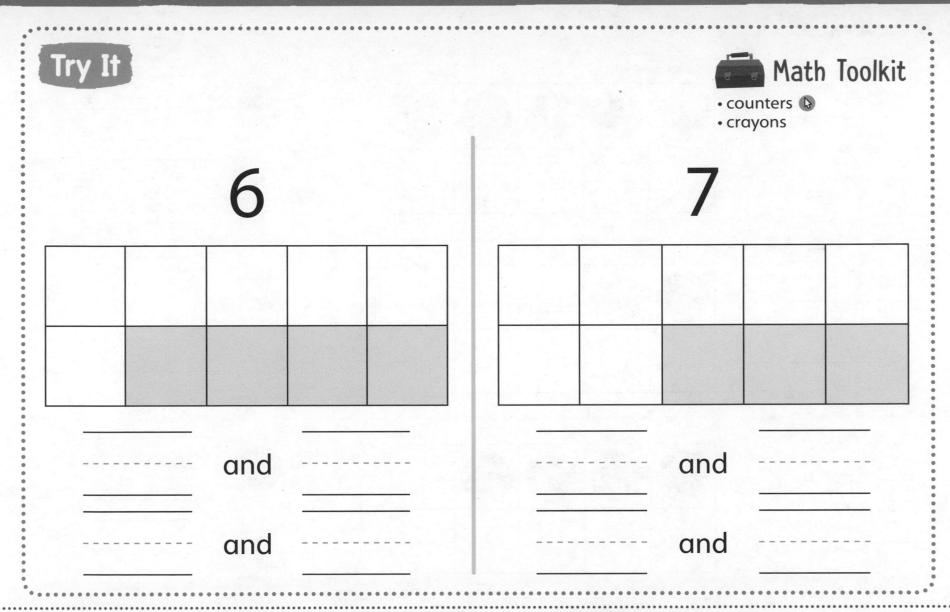

Try It

Math Toolkit
- counters
- crayons

6

7

_____ and _____

_____ and _____

_____ and _____

_____ and _____

Have children use counters to make 6 and then 7. Ask children to first find different number pairs that make 6 and write two ways. Then have them find number pairs that make 7 and write two ways.

Discuss It Can you make 7 using the same number of red counters and yellow counters? How can you be sure?

Connect It

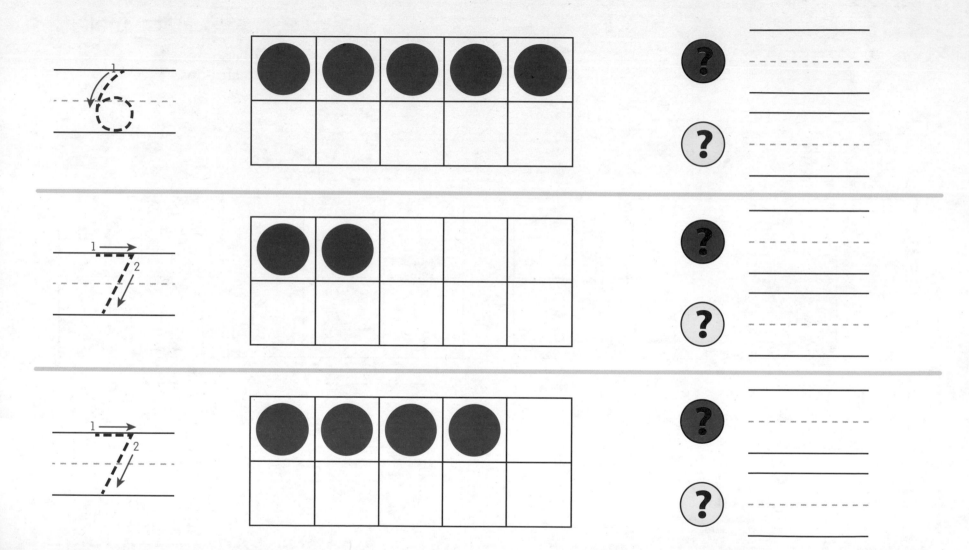

Ask children to draw counters in the 10-frames to make 6 or 7. Have children trace the total, then count and write the number of red and yellow counters they used to make the total.

Discuss It How can you tell how many counters you need to draw to finish a picture so that it shows 7?

Practice Making 6, 7, 8, and 9

Example

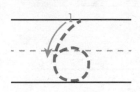
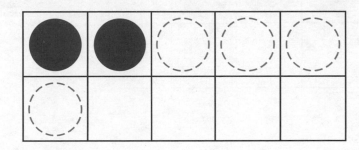
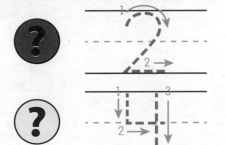

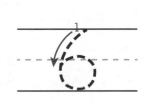
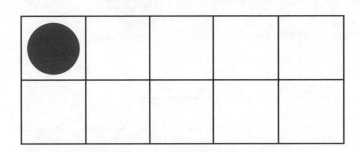
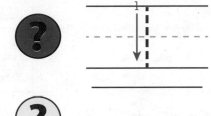

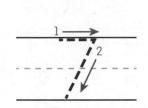

Have children trace the numbers on the left and draw more counters in the 10-frames to show a total of 6 or 7. On the right, have children write the number of red counters shown and the number of counters drawn to make the total.

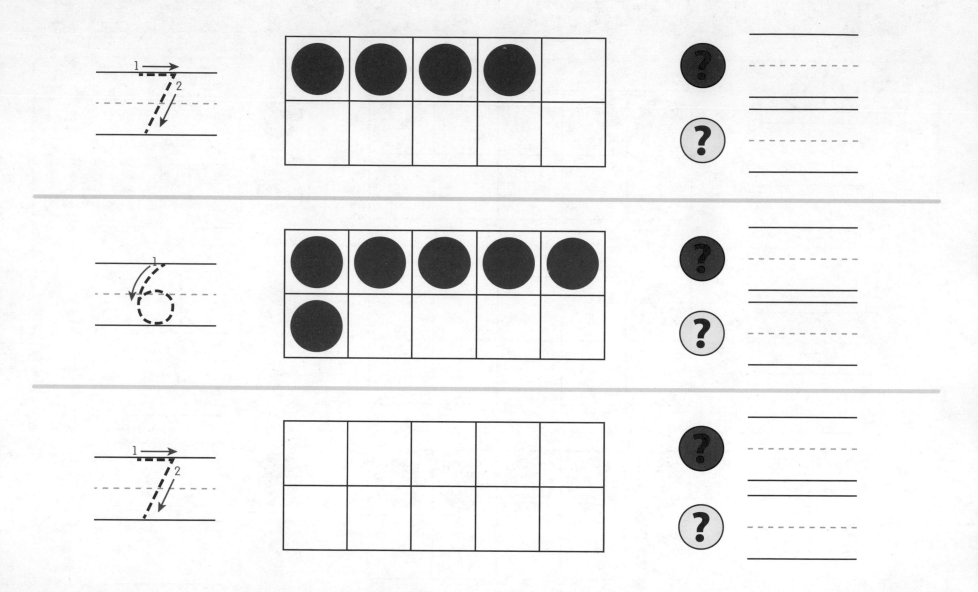

Have children trace the numbers on the left and draw more counters in the 10-frames (if needed) to make 6 or 7. For the first two problems, have children write the number of red counters shown and the number of counters drawn. For the last problem, ask children to use two colors to draw counters that show another way to make 7 and write the number pair.

Refine Making 6, 7, 8, and 9

Apply It

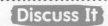 **Math Toolkit**
- two-color counters
- crayons

8

_____ and _____   _____ and _____

_____ and _____   _____ and _____

Have children use counters to make 8. Ask children to find 4 different number pairs that make 8 and write them.

Discuss It Do you think there are more than 4 ways to make 8? How can you be sure?

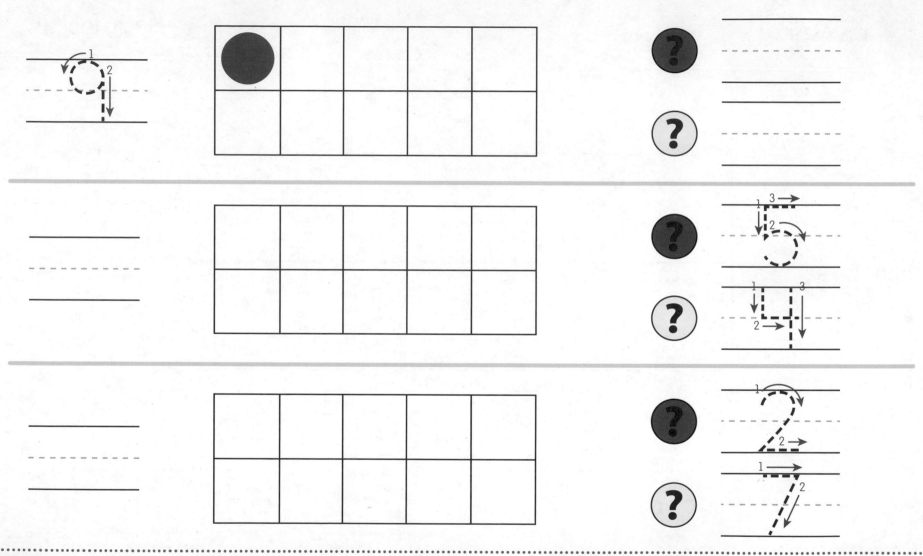

Ask children to show number pairs for 9 by drawing counters. For the first problem, have children complete the model and write the number of counters. For the last two problems, children use the given numbers to complete the model, then write the total.

Discuss It How is making 9 different from making 10?

Practice Making 6, 7, 8, and 9

Example

Have children draw counters in the 10-frames to make 8 or 9. Have children use the given number of counters to complete the model, then write the total to the left.

Have children draw counters in the 10-frames to make 8 or 9. For the first two problems, have children use the given number of counters to complete the model, then write the total to the left. For the last problem, ask children to use two colors to draw counters to show another way to make either 8 or 9, then write the number pair and the total to the left.

Refine Making 6, 7, 8, and 9

Apply It

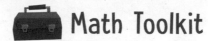 **Math Toolkit**
- two-color counters
- crayons

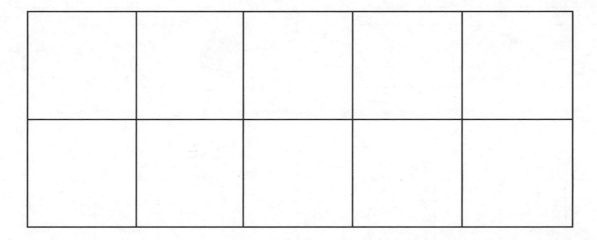

Have children use counters to show different ways to make 6, 7, 8, and 9. Ask children to show more than one way to make 9. Then ask them to show more than one way to make 6. Repeat for 7 and 8.

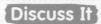 Do you think there are more ways to make 9 or 6? Why?

Make 6.

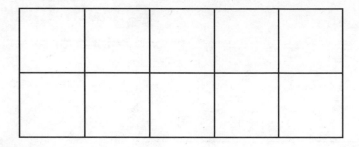

 ----------- **?** -----------

Make 9.

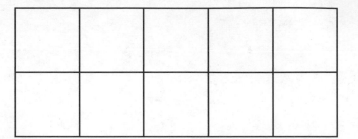

? ----------- -----------

Make 8.

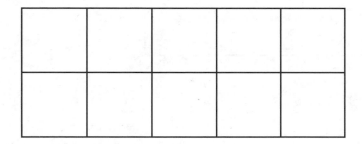

 ----------- **?** -----------

Make 7.

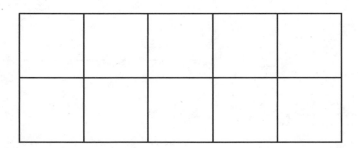

? ----------- -----------

Have children draw counters to make 6, 7, 8, and 9. Ask them to count and write the number of each color they use. Allow children to persevere in thinking about the possibilities.

Discuss It Work with a partner. Compare how you made each number. Did you use the same way? Different ways? Is each way correct?

Show What You Learned

Have children draw to show what they learned about numbers 6–10.
Prompt children to reflect on their learning by posing questions such as: *What* *mistake did you make that helped you learn? What did you work hardest to learn? What is the most important math you learned? Why?*

7

_____
- - - - -
_____

10

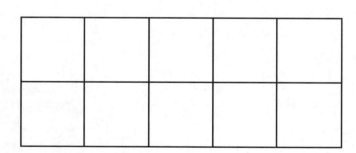

5 and 5

5 and 6

6 and 6

For the top problem, have children read the given number, look at the group of pails, and write the number of pails. For the bottom problem, have children circle the pair of numbers that makes 10. Children may choose to draw counters in the 10-frame to solve the problem.

Which is less?

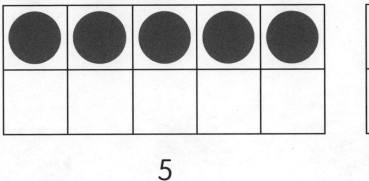

5

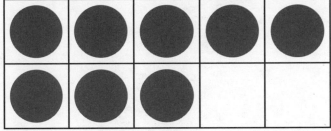

8

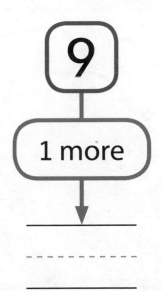

9

1 more

_____

- - - - - - - - -

_____

For the top problem, have children compare groups. Have children circle
the number that is less. For the bottom problem, have children write the
number that is one more than the given number.

Have children draw a box around the flowers, mark an X on the pails, and circle the shovels. Then have children count and write the number of each object shown.

Show What You Know

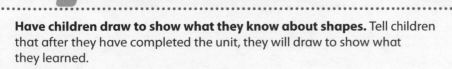

Have children draw to show what they know about shapes. Tell children that after they have completed the unit, they will draw to show what they learned.

Build Your Vocabulary

My Math Words

Shape	Name	My Picture
	circle	
	rectangle	
	square	
	triangle	

Have children look at each shape and say the name of the shape after you.
Then have children draw their own picture of each shape and color it using
colors of their choice.

Name Shapes

Dear Family,

This week your child is learning to name shapes.

Your child will also learn some of the ways to describe shapes. For example, **triangles, hexagons, rectangles, squares,** and **cubes** have **corners** and straight **sides**. A hexagon has 6 sides, and a square has 4 sides of equal length. **Circles, cylinders, spheres,** and **cones** have curves. Learning some of the ways to describe shapes will help your child identify and distinguish between different shapes.

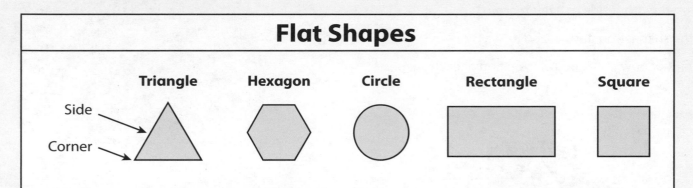

Flat Shapes

Triangle   Hexagon   Circle   Rectangle   Square

Side

Corner

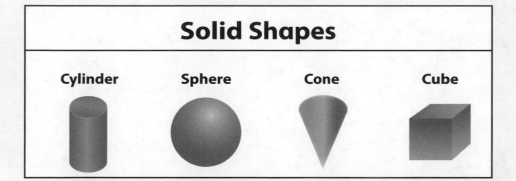

Solid Shapes

Cylinder   Sphere   Cone   Cube

Invite your child to share what he or she knows about naming shapes by doing the following activity together.

Activity Naming Shapes

Do this activity with your child to practice naming shapes.

Tell your child that you are going on a shape hunt.

- Together, look around your home and neighborhood for objects shaped like rectangles, squares, triangles, hexagons, and circles. In addition, look for objects shaped like cylinders, spheres, cones, and cubes. You may wish to bring this letter so that you can use the shapes on the other side as a reference.

- Encourage your child to name the shapes you find.

- You can make a chart to keep track of how many objects you find of each shape.

Explore Naming Shapes

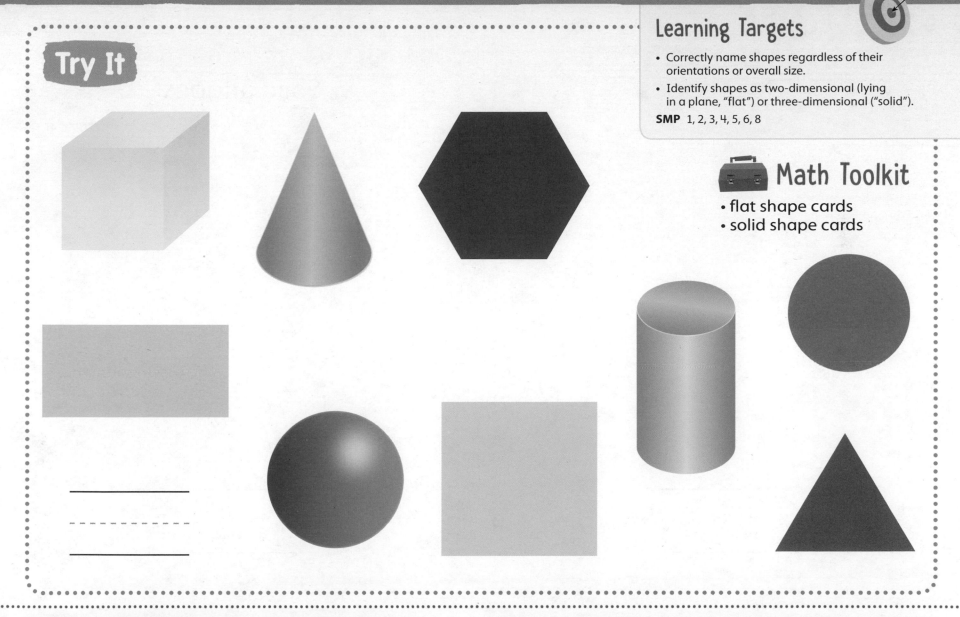

Try It

Learning Targets

- Correctly name shapes regardless of their orientations or overall size.
- Identify shapes as two-dimensional (lying in a plane, "flat") or three-dimensional ("solid").

SMP 1, 2, 3, 4, 5, 6, 8

Math Toolkit

- flat shape cards
- solid shape cards

Have children differentiate three-dimensional (solid) shapes from two-dimensional (flat) shapes and informally describe shapes. Display each shape pictured. Name each shape and have children repeat it. Have them informally describe each shape, including if it is flat or solid. Then name a shape and have children point to that shape above and tell if it is solid or flat. Then tell children to count and write the number of shapes shown.

Connect It

Flat Shapes

Solid Shapes

_____

- - - - - - -

_____

_____

- - - - - - -

_____

Have children identify shapes as flat or solid and name the shapes. Have pairs of children sort flat shape cards and solid shape cards and then name each of the shapes. Tell children to count the shapes they sorted and write the number of shapes in each group. Children then use a flat hand or a fist to identify objects they are shown as flat or solid.

Prepare for Naming Shapes

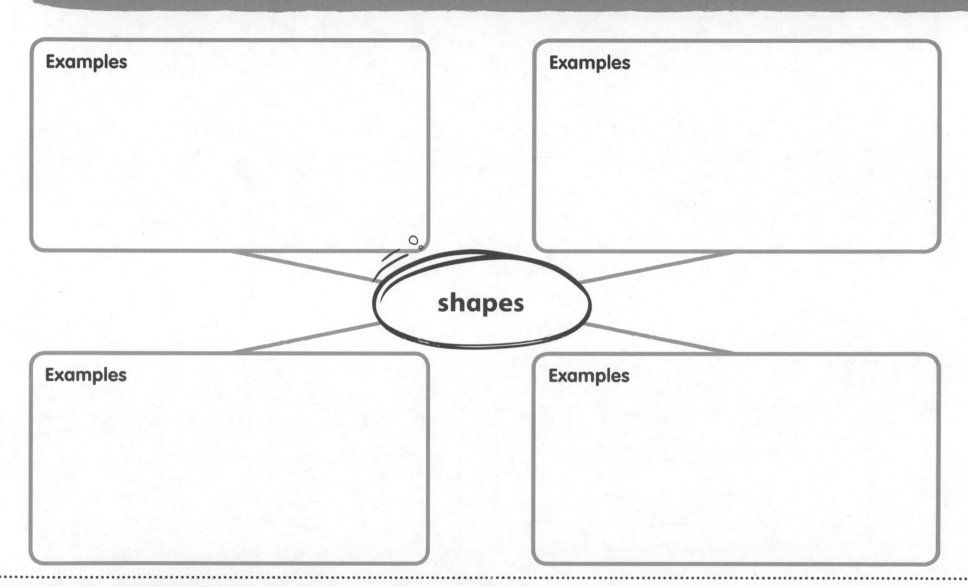

Examples

Examples

shapes

Examples

Examples

Have children show the meaning of the word *shapes*. Have children fill in each of the boxes to show the meaning of the word *shapes*. Tell children that they can use words, numbers, and pictures. Encourage them to show as many ideas as they can.

Flat Shapes

Solid Shapes

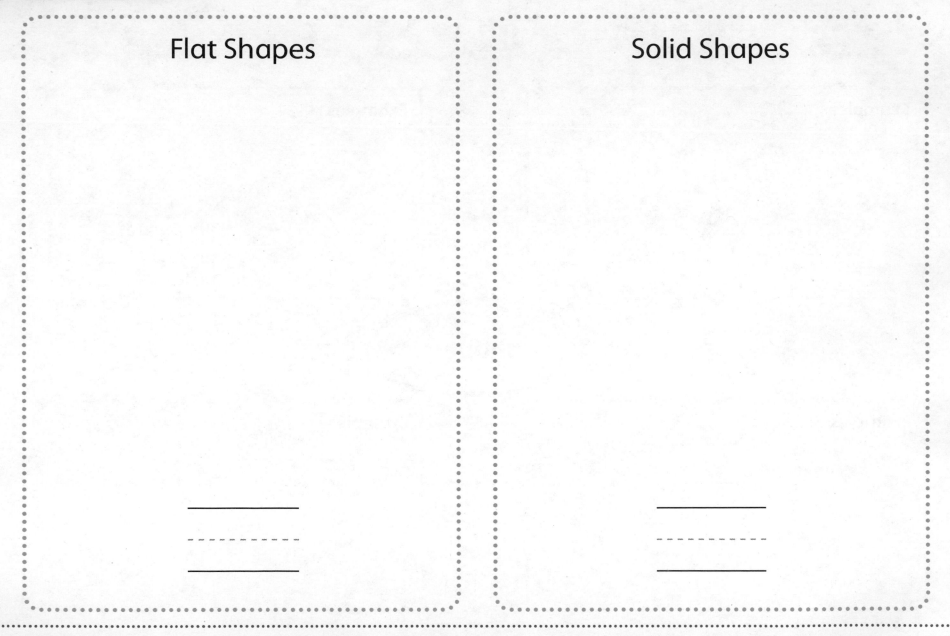

Have children identify shapes as flat or solid and name the shapes. Have children find objects with shapes they recognize and sort them into flat shapes and solid shapes and then name each of the shapes. Tell children to count the shapes they sorted and write the number of shapes in each group.

Develop Naming Shapes

Encourage children to describe the two- and three-dimensional shapes in the picture including squares, rectangles, circles, triangles, hexagons, spheres, cubes, cones, and cylinders. Have children ring (circle) one example of each solid shape.

Discuss It Which shapes are the easiest to find? Which shapes are the most difficult to find?

Connect It

🧰 Math Toolkit
• two- and three-
  dimensional shapes

Have children sort the shapes. For the top row, have children ring (circle) the flat shapes. For the middle row, have them ring the solid shapes. For the bottom row, have them ring the cylinders.

Discuss It How can you tell which shapes are flat? How can you tell which shapes are solid?

Practice Naming Shapes

Observe as you ask children to color different shapes on the page. Have children color a square, a rectangle, a circle, a triangle, and a hexagon. Then have children color a sphere, a cube, a cone, and a cylinder. Have children color the rest of the picture.

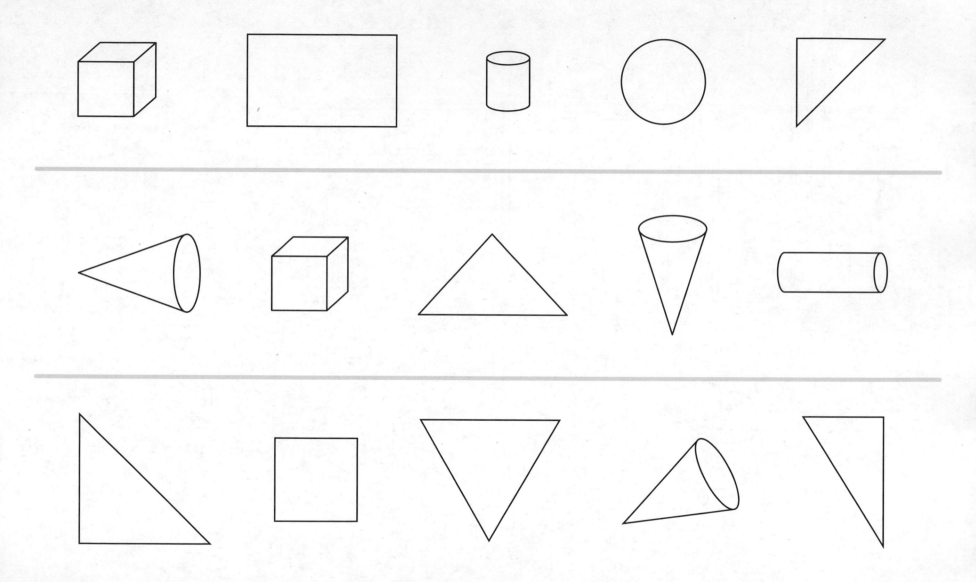

Ask children to identify and sort shapes into categories. Have children color all the flat shapes in the top row and all the solid shapes in the middle row. Then have children color all the triangles in the bottom row.

236   **Lesson 12** Name Shapes

Try It

Math Toolkit

• crayons

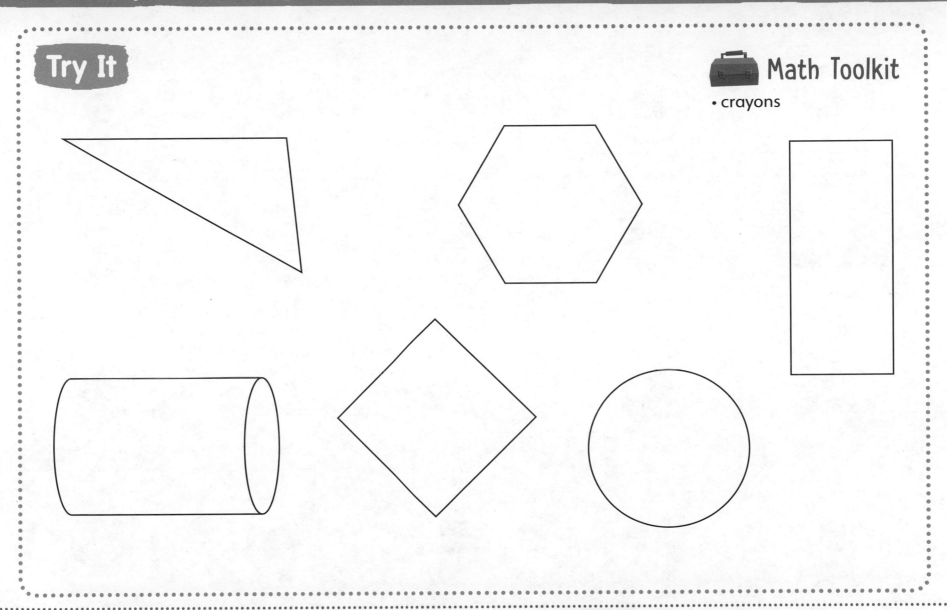

Have children identify flat shapes. Have children point to the shapes on the page as you name them: circle, triangle, rectangle, hexagon, and square. Then have them color the triangle yellow, hexagon red, square green, rectangle orange, and circle blue.

Discuss It How can you tell what a shape is by looking at it? Why has one shape not been colored?

Connect It

Ask children to distinguish flat shapes from solid shapes and then identify the flat shapes. Have children mark all the solid shapes with an X. Then have them ring (circle) the triangles purple, squares green, rectangles red, circles orange, and hexagons yellow.

Discuss It How would you describe a square to someone?

Practice Naming Shapes

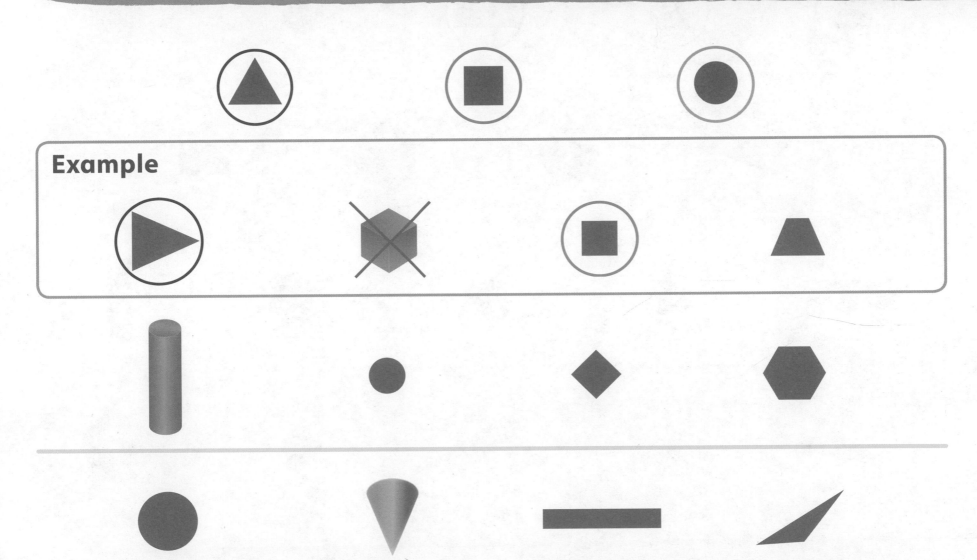

Example

Ask children to distinguish flat shapes from solid shapes and then identify the flat shapes. Have children mark all the solid shapes with an X.

Then have children ring (circle) the triangles red, the squares green, and the circles orange.

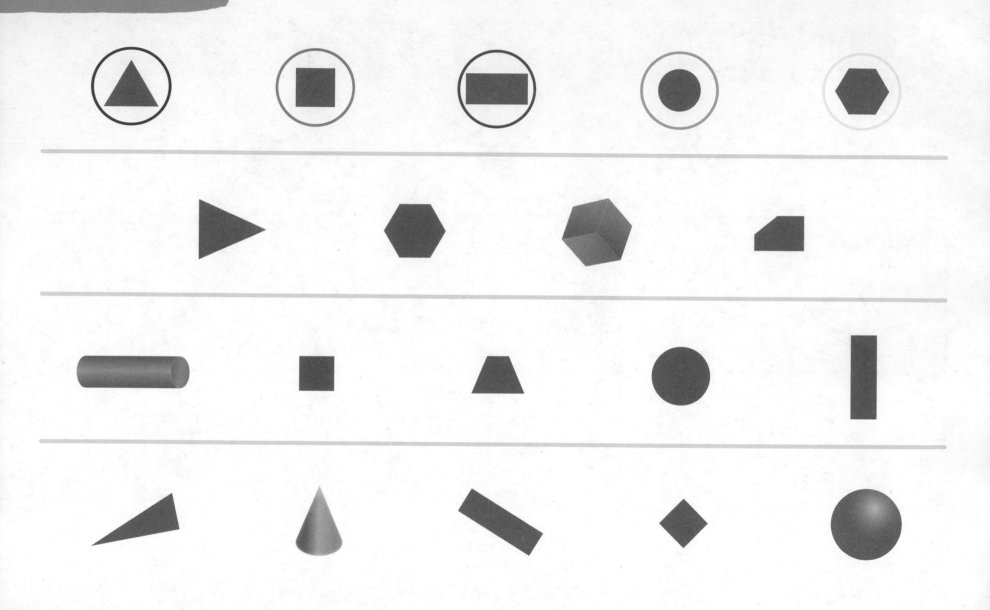

Ask children to distinguish flat shapes from solid shapes and then identify the flat shapes. Have children mark all the solid shapes with an X.

Then have children ring (circle) the triangles red, the squares green, the rectangles purple, the circles orange, and the hexagons yellow.

Refine Naming Shapes

Apply It

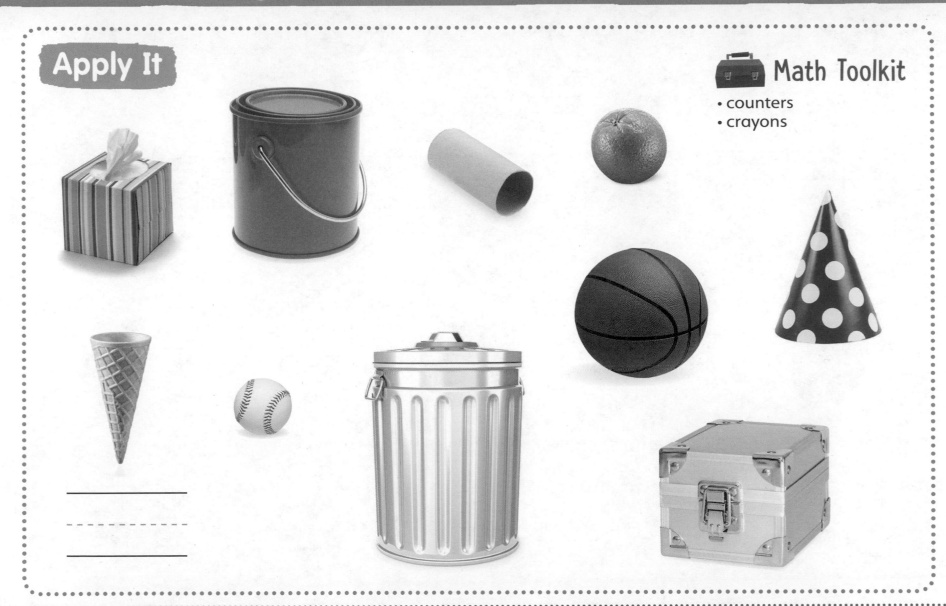

Math Toolkit
- counters
- crayons

_____
- - - - - - - - - - -
_____

Have children name and identify solid shapes. Ask children what shape the orange is and have them place counters on the other spheres. Repeat with the party hat, can of paint, and tissue box. Then have children count and write the number of objects shown.

 How can you tell the different solid shapes apart?

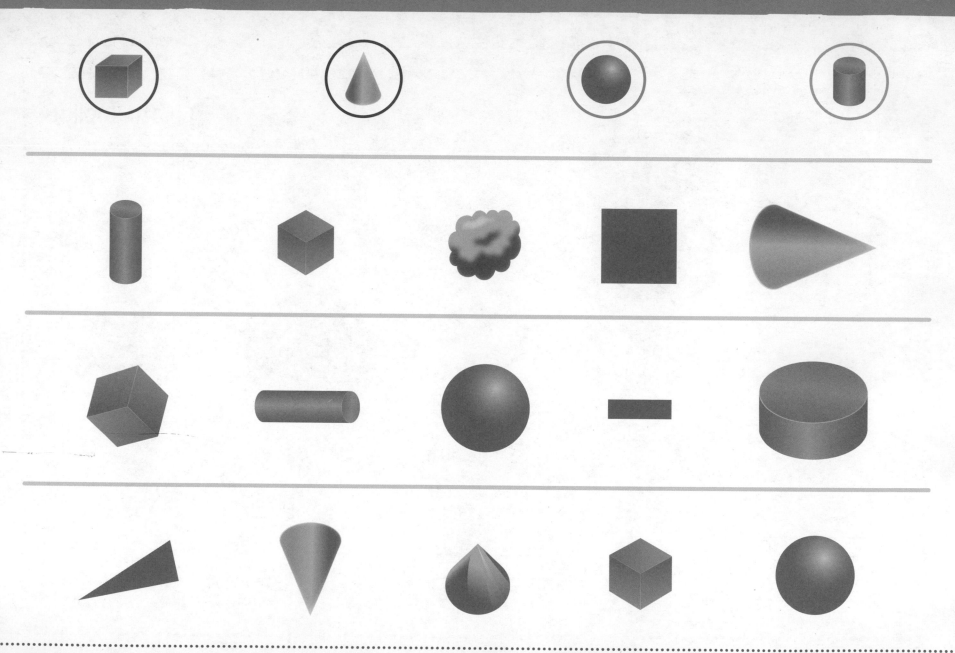

Ask children to distinguish flat shapes from solid shapes and then identify the solid shapes. Have children mark all the flat shapes with an X. Then have them ring (circle) the cubes purple, cones red, spheres green, and cylinders orange.

Discuss It What shape makes the top of a cube?

Practice Naming Shapes

Example

Ask children to distinguish flat shapes from solid shapes and then identify the solid shapes. Have children mark all the flat shapes with an X. Then have children ring (circle) the cubes purple, the cones red, the spheres green, and the cylinders orange.

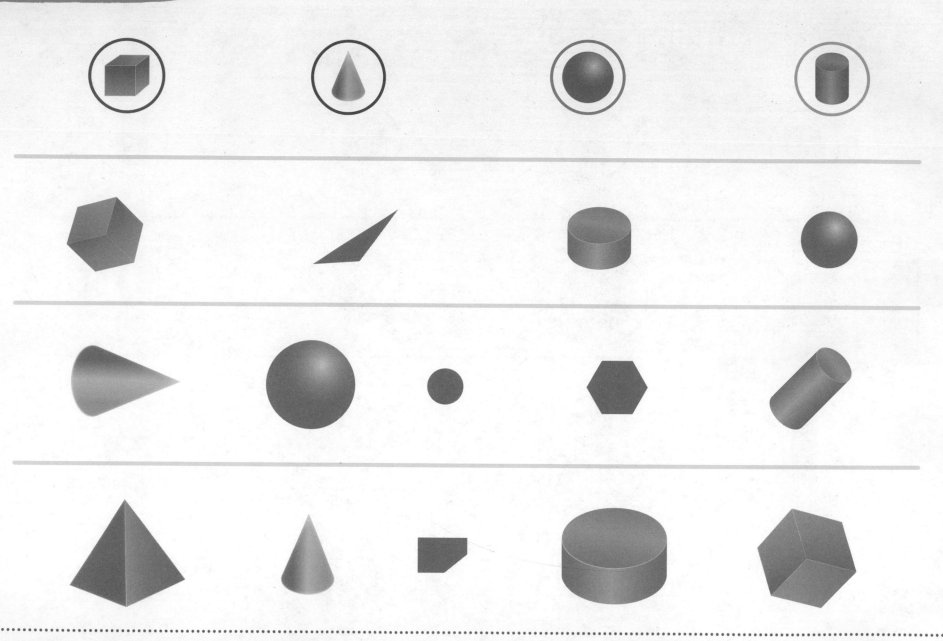

Ask children to distinguish flat shapes from solid shapes and then identify the solid shapes. Have children mark all the flat shapes with an X.

Then have children ring (circle) the cubes purple, the cones red, the spheres green, and the cylinders orange.

Refine Naming Shapes

Apply It

Math Toolkit

• crayons

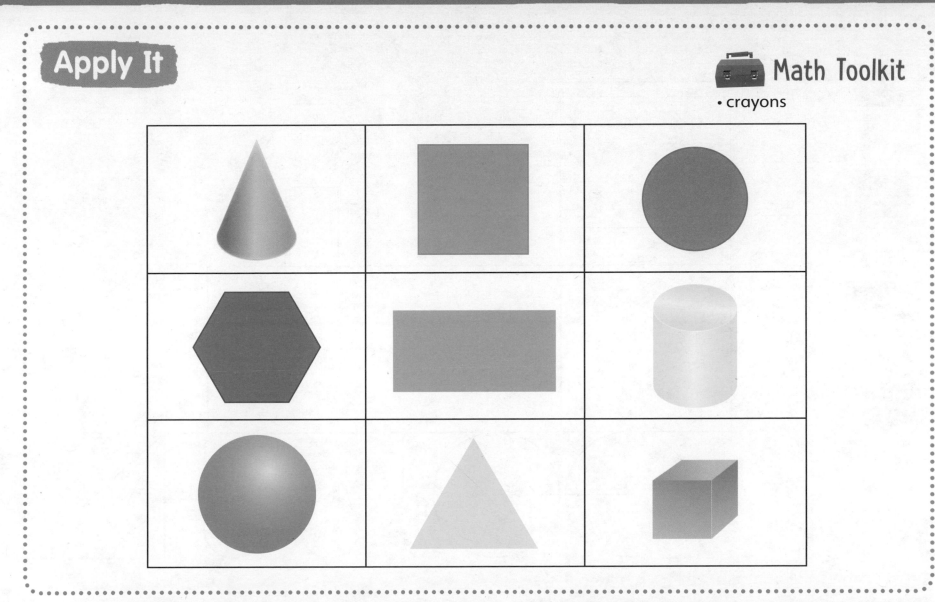

Have children match flat and solid shapes to a description. Prepare a bag of shapes with a circle, square, rectangle, triangle, hexagon, cube, cone, cylinder, and sphere. Ask a child to take a shape from the bag and describe it. Children ring that shape. Repeat.

Discuss It  What objects could you put in the bag instead of shape blocks to match the shapes on the page?

Have children color the shapes in the picture using the colors at the side of the page.
Remind children to look for different kinds of rectangles and triangles.

Discuss It How many of each shape did you find?

See Position and Shape

Dear Family,

This week your child is learning to recognize the position and shape of objects.

Position language such as **above, below, beside, in front of, behind,** and **next to** is used to describe the location of objects.

There are many different shapes that can be seen within real-world objects. Recognizing shapes in his or her environment will help your child prepare for upcoming geometry lessons about shape attributes such as sides and corners.

Triangle **Square** **Rectangle** **Circle**

Cylinder **Cone** **Sphere** **Cube**

Invite your child to share what he or she knows about recognizing position and shape by doing the following activity together.

Activity Seeing Position and Shape

Do this activity with your child to practice recognizing positions and shapes.

• Play an "I Spy" game focusing on the position and shape of household objects. Describe where you see a shape and have your child try to find it. You might walk around to different rooms in the house, or you may choose to gather a collection of objects to display together in ways that demonstrate position words such as *above, below, beside, in front of, behind*, and *next to*.

• For example, to describe a clock, you might say: *I spy a circle above a bookshelf*. Your child looks around to try to find the circle you are thinking of. If your child guesses a different circle, you can say something like: *That is a circle, but it is not the circle I picked. The circle I picked is above a bookshelf*. Have your child continue to guess until he or she finds the object you described.

• Take turns asking and answering "I Spy" questions about household objects shaped like squares, rectangles, triangles, circles, cubes, cones, cylinders, and/or spheres. Household objects you might refer to include napkins, doors, shapes on food packages, plates, toy blocks, ice cream cones, soup cans, and balls.

I spy a cylinder next to a paper bag.

Explore Seeing Position and Shape

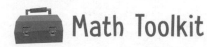

Learning Target

- Describe objects in the environment using names of shapes, and describe the relative positions of these objects using terms such as *above, below, beside, in front of, behind,* and *next to.*

SMP 1, 2, 3, 4, 5, 6

Math Toolkit

- counters

Children are introduced to position words and place objects in different positions. Introduce children to position words by pointing to different objects in the room and describing them as *above, below, beside, in front of, behind,* or *next to* another object. Ask children to use position words to describe the position of one child relative to another child. Then have children place a counter in a position as described relative to Snargg.

Connect It

Children draw pictures positioned as described relative to the camper and act out position words. Have children draw pictures positioned relative to the camper as described. Say: *Draw a star below the camper*. Then play

Teacher Says, a variation of Simon Says, as a class to act out positions. Say: *Teacher says, place your hand above your head*. Occasionally omit the phrase "Teacher says" before the instruction.

Prepare for Seeing Position and Shape

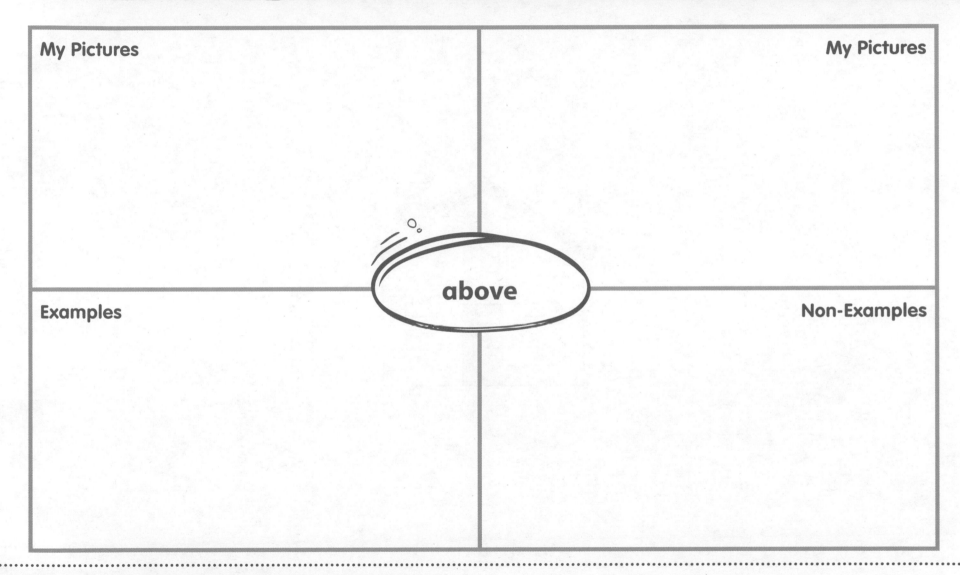

My Pictures	My Pictures
Examples	**Non-Examples**

above

Have children complete as many boxes as they can. Have children draw pictures to show the meaning of the word *above*. Then have children draw or write examples and non-examples of the word *above*.

Have children practice position words. Have children draw pictures positioned relative to the house as described, such as: *Draw a sun above the house. Draw a flower below a window.*

Develop Seeing Position and Shape

Encourage children to describe shapes and the position of objects. Have children use words such as *above, below, beside; in front of, behind,* and *next to.* Have children ring (circle) an object next to the dog.

 **Discuss It** What shapes do you see in the picture?

Have children find objects based on their position. Have children draw a ring (circle) around the object above the jackets, draw a line under the object in front of the red bowl, and mark with an X two objects behind the table.

Discuss It How can you describe where the backpack is in the picture? How can you describe where the yellow jacket is?

Practice Seeing Position and Shape

Observe as you ask children to color different objects on the page. Have children color the child with the book, the child in front of him, and a window above the child with the book. Then have children color the child next to the squirrel, the leaves below the safety cone, and one object above the bus. Tell children to color the rest of the picture.

Ask children to ring (circle) the flowers beside the bench and color the flower below the tree purple. Have children color the object in front of a bench red and the boat behind the sailboat blue. You may then wish to allow children to color the rest of the picture.

Develop Seeing Position and Shape

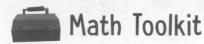
Math Toolkit
• attribute blocks
• geometric solids

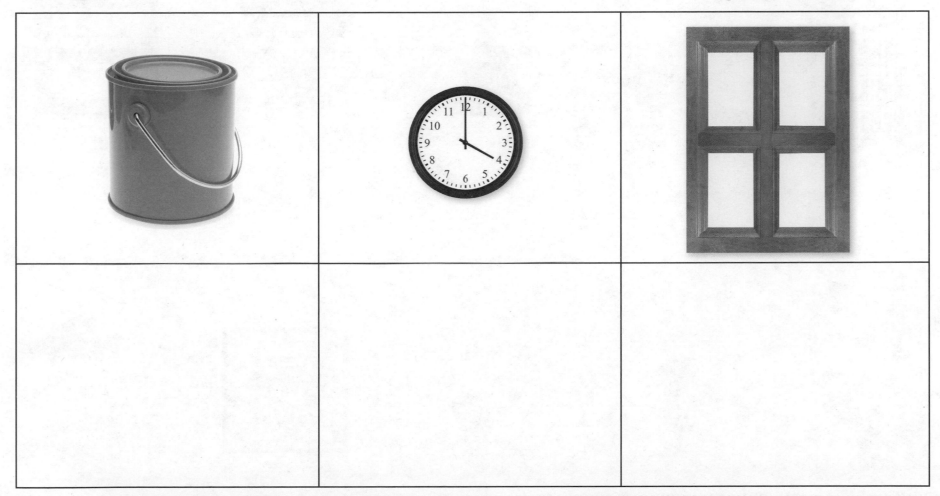

Have children find similar shapes in the classroom. Hold up a cylinder. Ask children to find another object in the classroom that has a similar shape, use a position word to describe its position, and draw it underneath the can. Repeat with a circle and a rectangle.

 Look again at the object you found. How is its shape similar to the object on the page?

Connect It

Have children match the shapes with the same name. Have children draw lines to connect the objects with the same shape and then name the shape. Use real objects to help children recognize that orientation and size do not change the name used to describe the shape.

Discuss It How did you decide which objects match?

Practice Seeing Position and Shape

Example

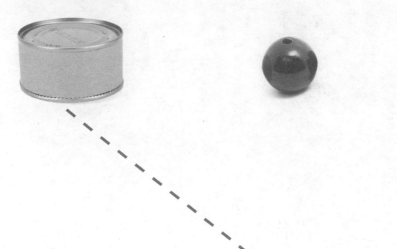

Have children match shapes with the same name. Have children draw lines to connect the objects with the same shape and then name the shapes.

Use real objects to prompt children to recognize that position and size do not change the name used to describe the shape.

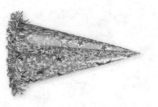

Have children match shapes with the same name. Have children draw lines to connect the objects with the same shape and then name the shapes.

Use real objects to prompt children to recognize that position and size do not change the name used to describe the shape.

Refine Seeing Position and Shape

Apply It

Have children draw objects in positions related to a sheet of paper. Have them place a sheet of paper on the desk. Have them put objects in the following places and then draw them: pencil next to, crayon below, eraser above, marker beside, and scissors in front of.

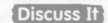 Place a glue stick behind the paper. Why are you unable to see the glue stick?

Ask children to identify objects that are below, behind, beside, or above. Have children ring (circle) the pictures where the leaf is below the can and the ball is behind the dog. Then have them ring the person beside the dog and the object above the bus.

Discuss It What shapes can you see in these pictures?

Practice Seeing Position and Shape

Example

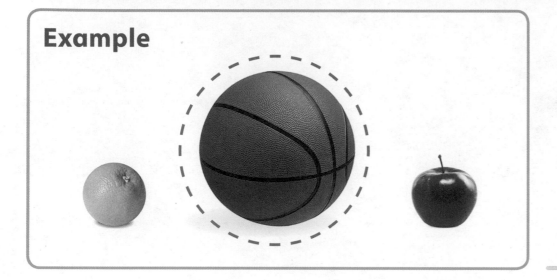

Ask children to identify objects that are next to, above, behind, or below. Have children ring (circle) the object that is next to the apple and the trash can with the leaf above it. Then have children ring (circle) the animal that is behind the dog and the acorn that is below the bench.

Ask children to identify objects that are above, behind, in front of, or beside. Have children ring (circle) the animal above the squirrel and the object behind the milk. Then have children ring (circle) the object in front of the bus and the object beside the tree.

Refine Seeing Position and Shape

Apply It

 Math Toolkit
- object cards

Have children sit in chairs and follow directions to place objects. Direct children to take an object, name its shape, and hold it in different positions. For example: *Place the box below your chair.* Have children paste their shapes on the page to show what they acted out.

 How do you know where to paste the shapes on the page?

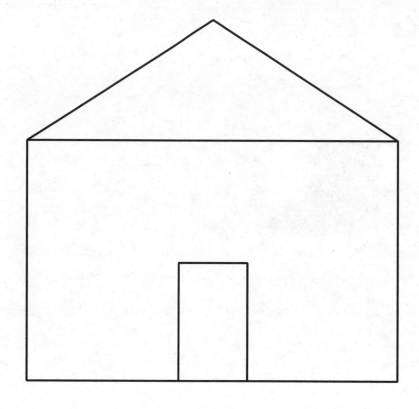

Have children draw shapes and objects from verbal instructions. Have children draw a cloud above the house, a flower in front of the house, a boy next to the house, a window beside the door, a circle above the door, a rock below the window, and a tree behind the dog.

 Work with a partner. Are the locations of the objects in your drawings the same? How are they different?

Compare Shapes

Dear Family,

This week your child is learning to compare shapes.

In order to compare shapes, you need to think about their attributes. For example, the cylinders, cones, and spheres below are alike because they are solid shapes that can roll.

Some solid shapes are alike because they can stack, such as the three shapes below. The first and third shapes, which are cubes, are most alike because they each have 6 square faces. A flat surface of a solid shape is called a **face**.

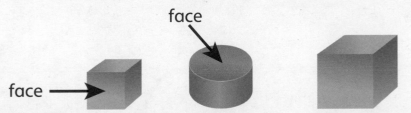

face

face

When comparing flat shapes, such as those below, you can compare the number of sides and the lengths of sides. For example, each shape below has 4 sides. But only the first and third shapes, which are squares, have all sides of equal length.

Invite your child to share what he or she knows about comparing shapes by doing the following activity together.

Activity Comparing Shapes

Do this activity with your child to compare shapes.

Materials 1 household object shaped like a cylinder (such as a food can), 1 household object shaped like a cube (such as a toy block or cube-shaped tissue box), 1 household object shaped like a sphere (such as a ball), paper and pencil

Place the objects shaped like a cylinder, cube, and sphere on the floor for your child (so that you do not have to worry about objects rolling off the table). Ask him or her questions about the shapes, such as the following:

1. *Which shapes roll?*

2. *Which shapes stack?*

3. *Which shape has corners?*

4. *Which shape has faces that are squares?*

5. *Which shape has faces that are circles?*

Have your child hold the cylinder and then the cube on a sheet of paper while you trace around one face of each object. Ask your child to name the flat shapes you drew (circle and square) and tell you how they are alike and different. Encourage your child to use the circle and square to make a drawing or design.

Answers: **1.** cylinder and sphere; **2.** cylinder and cube; **3.** cube; **4.** cube; **5.** cylinder

Explore Comparing Shapes

Try It

Learning Target

- Analyze and compare two- and three-dimensional shapes, in different sizes and orientations, using informal language to describe their similarities, differences, parts and other attributes.

SMP 1, 2, 3, 4, 5, 6, 7

Math Toolkit

- attribute blocks
- geometric solids

Have children play a game to identify attributes that shapes have in common. Give each child a flat or solid shape. Hold up a cube. Describe an attribute of the cube and have children raise their hands if their shape has that attribute. Choose a child to identify the attribute on his or her shape. Then that child describes a different attribute. Repeat with other children. Then have children sort a cube, cylinder, circle, and square based on attributes you describe.

Connect It

Have children draw shapes. Ask children to draw a square on one side of the page. Have them explain how they know they drew a square. Then have children draw a circle on the other side of the page. Ask them to explain how they know the shape they drew is a circle.

Prepare for Comparing Shapes

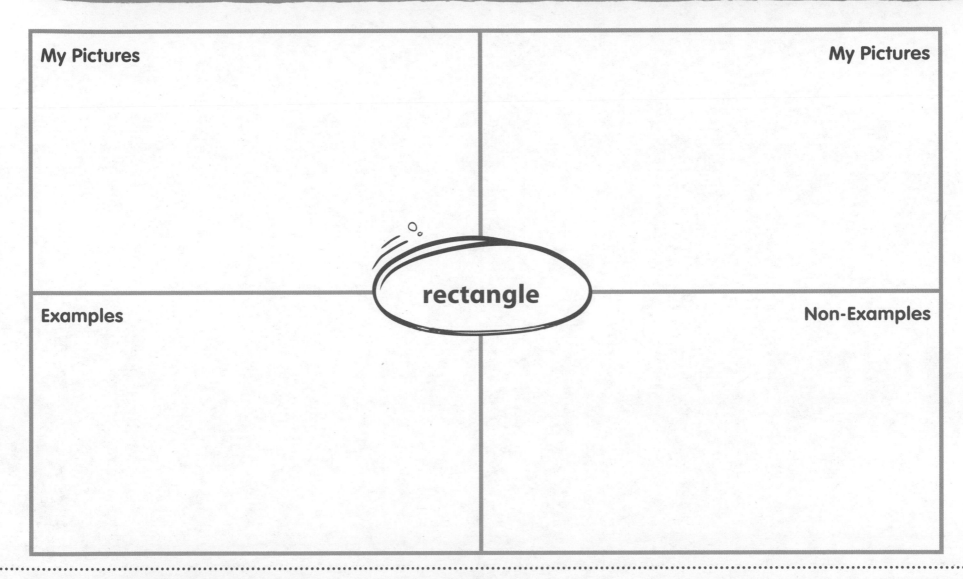

My Pictures	My Pictures
Examples	**Non-Examples**

rectangle

Have children complete as many boxes as they can. Have children draw pictures to show the meaning of the word *rectangle*. Then have children draw examples and non-examples of rectangles.

Have children draw shapes. Ask children to draw a triangle on one side of the page. Have them explain how they know they drew a triangle. Then have children draw a rectangle on the other side of the page. Ask them to explain how they know the shape they drew is a rectangle.

Develop Comparing Shapes

Encourage children to look for shapes that are alike in some way and to describe how they are alike. Encourage children to talk about curves, corners, or the number or length of sides. Have children ring (circle) all the solid shapes that can roll.

Discuss It What objects can you see in your classroom that have a shape like the shape of the paint cans?

Connect It

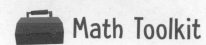 Math Toolkit

- attribute blocks
- geometric solids

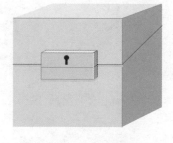

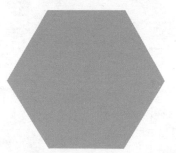

Have children look for shapes that are alike in some way. Have children ring (circle) all the shapes that do not have curves. Then have them mark with an X all solids that have faces that are circles.

Discuss It How would you describe a cylinder or cone? What words could you use?

Practice Comparing Shapes

Direct children's attention to the shapes poster below the clock. Have children color all the shapes with 3 sides. Then direct children's attention to the top shelf. Tell children to color the shapes that have corners using one color and shapes that have no corners using another color. Have children color the rest of the picture.

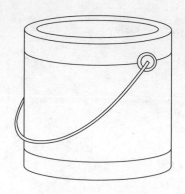

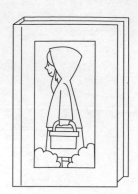

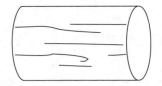

Ask children to look for shapes that are alike in some way. Have children color all the shapes that have corners red. Then have children color all solid shapes that have faces that are circles blue.

276   Lesson 14 Compare Shapes

Develop Comparing Shapes

 Try It

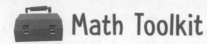 Math Toolkit

- straws
- clay

Have children make and draw triangles. Give children cut straws of different lengths and small clay balls. Have children use three straws joined by clay to make a triangle. Have children make two more triangles and then draw them all on the page.

 Discuss It What is the same about each triangle? What is different? How do you know when you have made a triangle?

Connect It

Have children ring (circle) the two shapes that are most alike. Have children focus their attention on the number of sides, the types of corners, or sides that are the same length. Ask children to describe both what is alike and what is different.

 Discuss It Which shapes on the page are different from all the others? Describe how they are different.

Practice Comparing Shapes

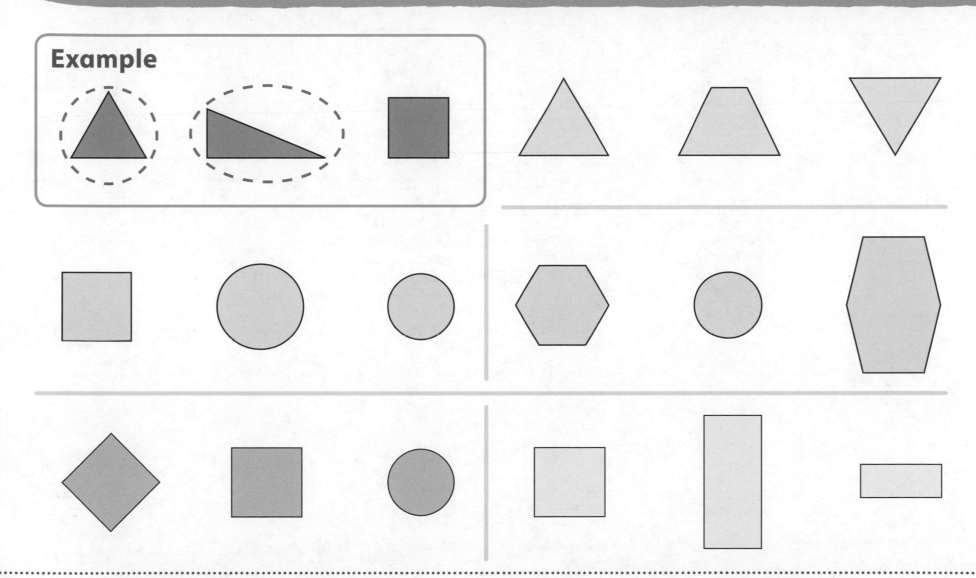

Example

Have children ring (circle) the two shapes that are most alike. Have children focus their attention on the number of sides, the types of corners, or sides that are the same length. Ask children to describe both what is alike and what is different.

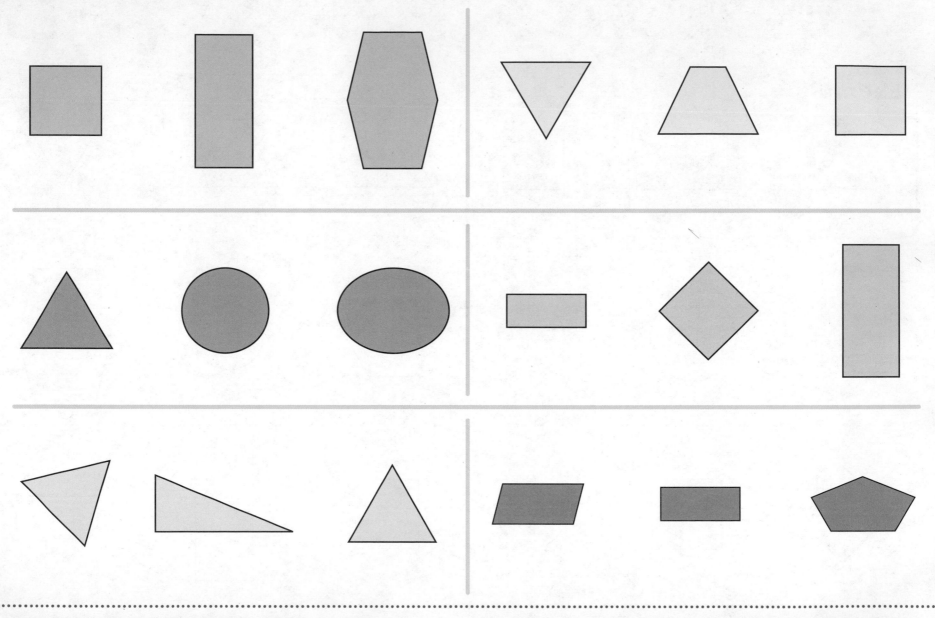

Have children ring (circle) the two shapes that are most alike. Have children focus their attention on the number of sides, the types of corners, or sides that are the same length. Ask children to describe both what is alike and what is different.

Refine Comparing Shapes

Apply It

Have children match shapes with the same attributes. Point to one of the shapes. Ask: *Can you find the same shape? How do you know they are the same?* Repeat with other shapes. Have children draw lines to match all the shapes.

Discuss It What parts of a shape can you look at to see if two shapes are the same?

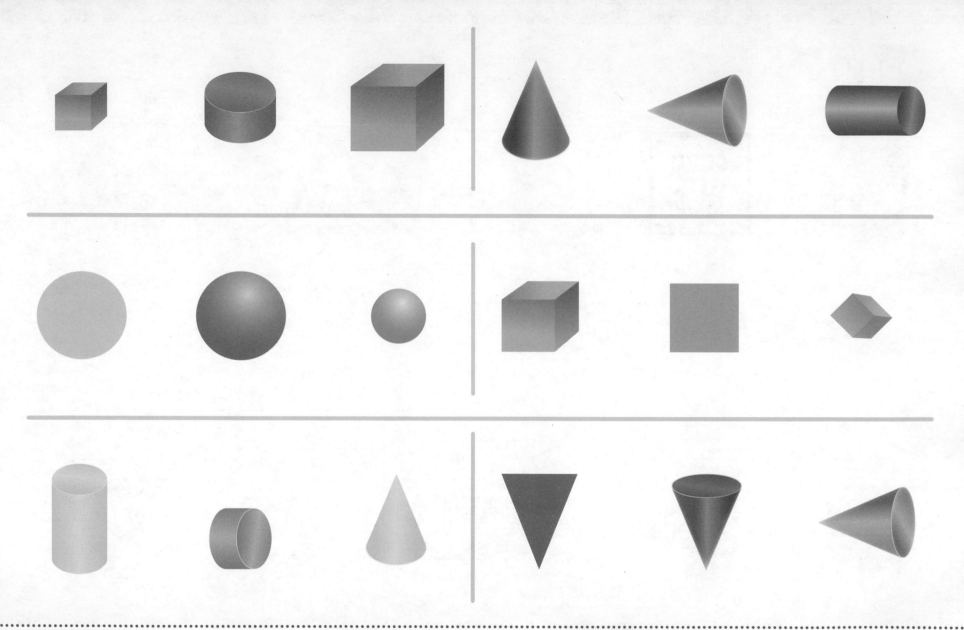

Have children ring (circle) the two shapes that are most alike. Have children focus their attention on whether the shapes are flat or solid and the kind of solid. Ask children to describe both what is alike and what is different.

Discuss It For each group, describe how the shape you did not ring is different from the other two shapes.

Practice Comparing Shapes

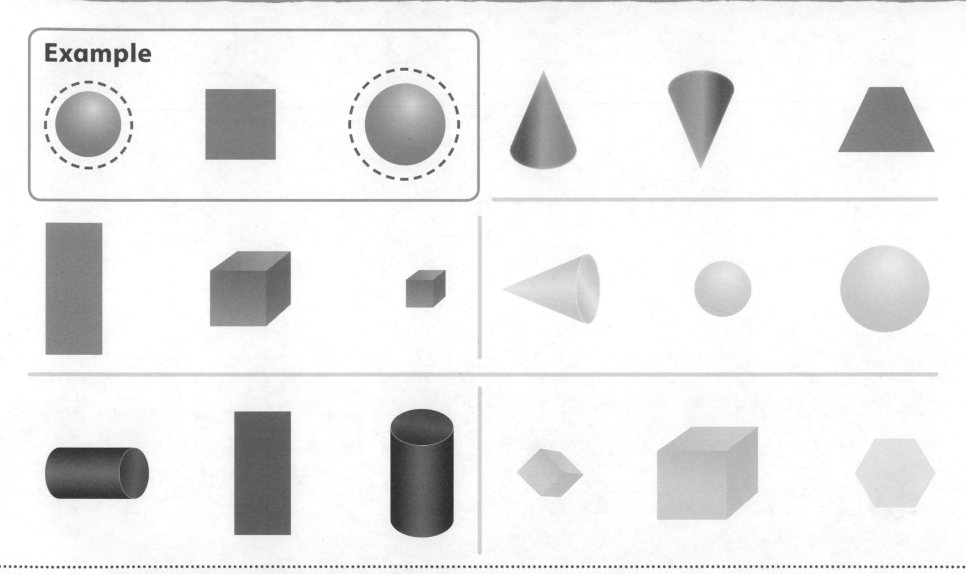

Example

Have children ring (circle) the two shapes that are most alike. Have children focus their attention on whether the shapes are flat or solid and the kind of solid. Ask children to describe both what is alike and what is different.

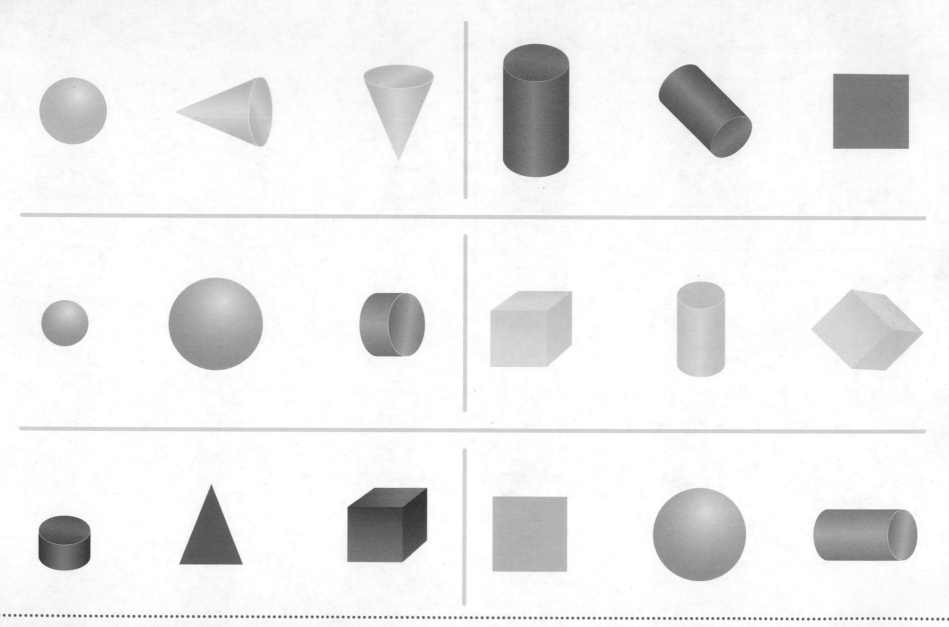

Have children ring (circle) the two shapes that are most alike. Have children focus their attention on whether the shapes are flat or solid and the kind of solid. Ask children to describe both what is alike and what is different.

Refine Comparing Shapes

Apply It

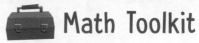 **Math Toolkit**

- attribute blocks
- flat shape cards
- solid shape cards

Have children sort shapes by attribute. Give children a set of attribute blocks or cut out shapes. Say an attribute, such as *3 sides*. Have them place the shapes with that attribute on the workmat. Clear the workmat and repeat using other attributes.

 **Discuss It** What other ways could you sort the shapes into a group?

4 sides

☐ face

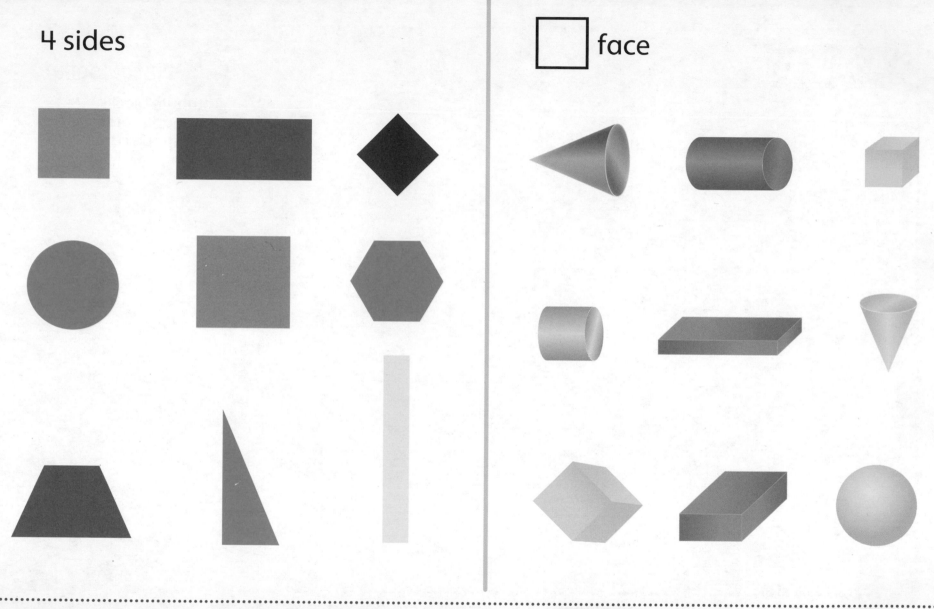

Have children analyze the flat shapes and solids and look for those with the given attribute. On the left, have children ring (circle) figures with four sides. On the right, have children ring (circle) solids with a square face.

Discuss It How did you decide which shapes to ring?

Build Shapes

Dear Family,

This week your child is learning to build shapes.

Shapes can be put together to form larger shapes. For example, two squares can be put together to form a rectangle.

Also, two triangles can be put together to form a square, and four triangles can be put together to form a rectangle.

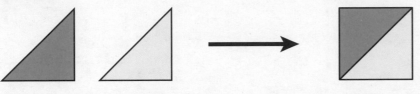

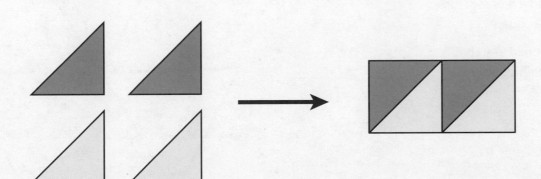

Learning to place shapes side by side to form larger shapes will help your child build a foundation for work in later grades with equal parts, fractions, area, and volume. Invite your child to share what he or she knows about building shapes by doing the following activity together.

Activity Building Shapes

Do this activity with your child to build shapes.

Materials 12 or more toothpicks (or other straight objects such as small craft sticks or straws cut into same-size pieces)

Ask your child to use some of the toothpicks to build a square. Then, providing assistance as needed, have your child add toothpicks to show how a rectangle can be built from two squares.

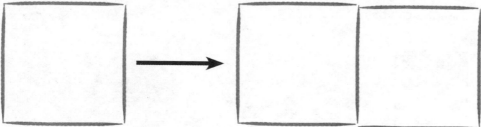

For an additional challenge, ask your child to build a rectangle from 3 squares and to build a large square from 4 small squares.

Then have your child put toothpicks together to build any shape, picture, or design. If you wish, help your child glue his or her toothpick arrangement to a sheet of paper.

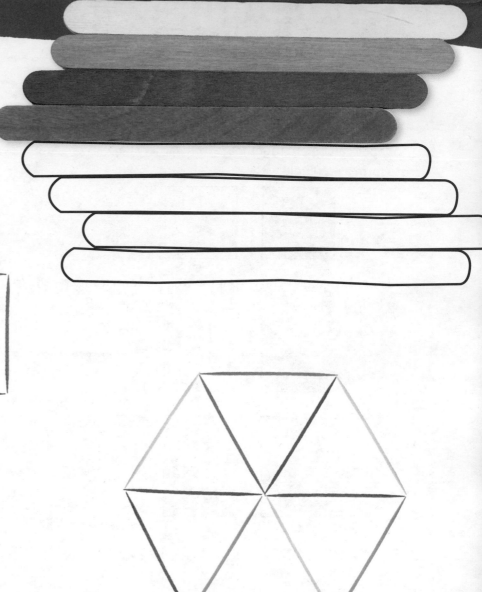

Explore Building Shapes

Learning Targets

- Model shapes in the world by building shapes from components and drawing shapes.
- Compose simple shapes to form larger shapes.

SMP 1, 2, 3, 4, 5, 6, 7

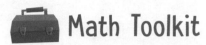 **Math Toolkit**

- triangles and squares

Have children put together shapes to make squares and rectangles. Give children 4 right triangles and 4 squares. Ask: *Which shapes can you put together to make a square?* Have children arrange shapes on the workmat to make a square.

Invite children to share how they combined shapes. Repeat, asking: *Which shapes can you use to make a rectangle? How can you use triangles to make a rectangle?*

Connect It

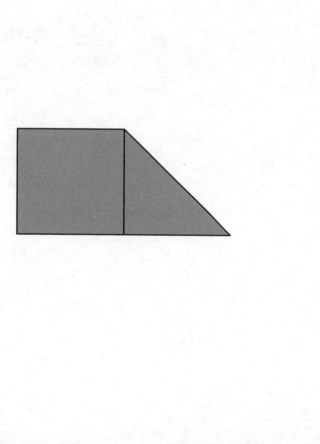

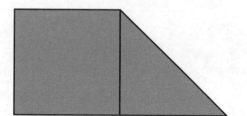

Have children add shapes to an existing shape to make a rectangle and then a triangle. Ask: *How can I add another shape to make this shape a rectangle?* Have children add one shape to the shape on the page to make a rectangle. Invite children to explain how to make a rectangle. Then ask: *How can I add another shape to make this shape a triangle?* Have children add one shape to make a triangle and explain how.

Prepare for Building Shapes

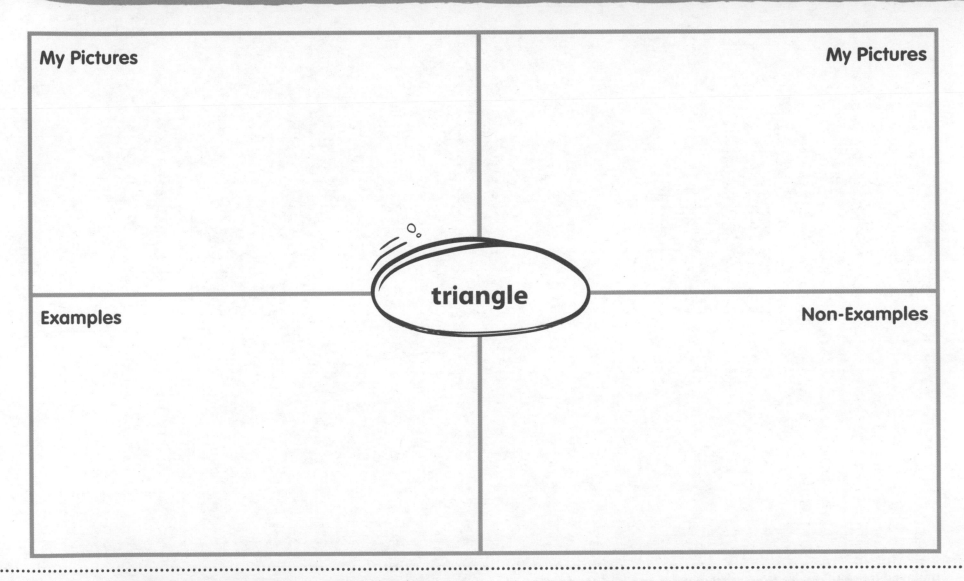

My Pictures	My Pictures
Examples	**Non-Examples**

(center: **triangle**)

Have children complete as many boxes as they can. Have children draw pictures to show the meaning of the word *triangle*. Then have children draw examples and non-examples of triangles.

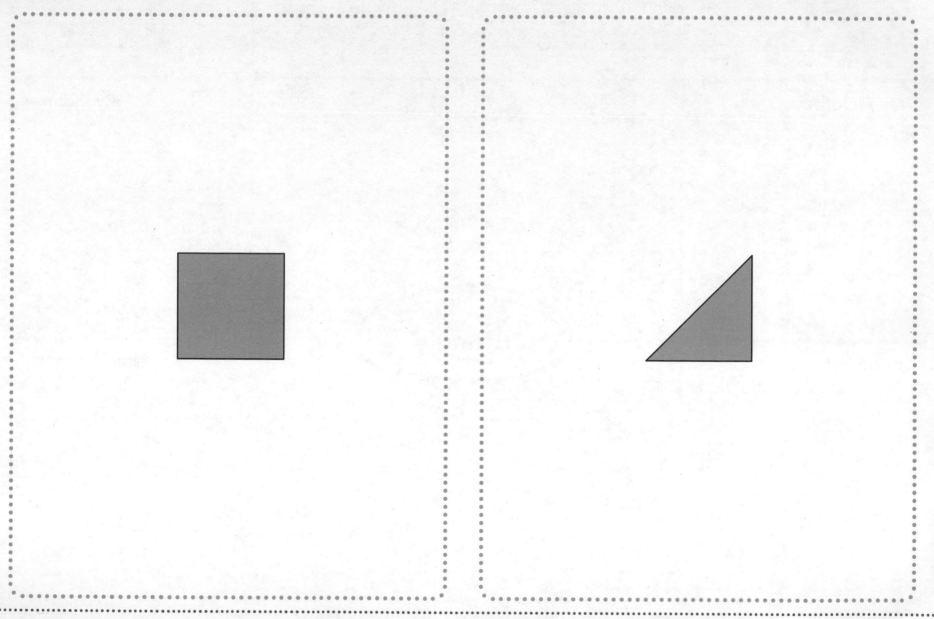

Have children add shapes to an existing shape to make a rectangle and then a triangle. Ask: *How can I add another shape to make this square a rectangle?* Have children add one shape to the square to make a rectangle.

Invite children to explain how to make a rectangle. Then ask: *How can I add another shape to make this triangle a bigger triangle?* Have children add one shape to make a bigger triangle and explain how.

292   Lesson 15 Build Shapes

Develop Building Shapes

Encourage children to name small shapes within bigger shapes. Ask children to find several examples, such as the small rectangles in the fence that make up the larger rectangle. Have children find and ring (circle) two squares that make a rectangle.

Discuss It What different shapes can you make when you put two triangles together?

Connect It

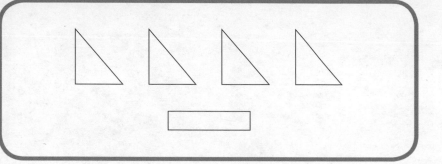

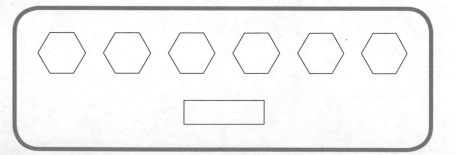

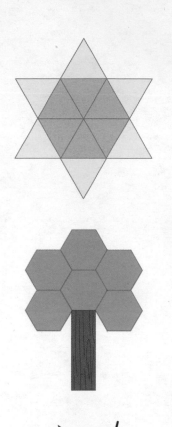

Have children find small shapes within a larger shape. Have children look at the different shapes used to make each object. Then have them draw lines to match each group of smaller shapes to the object they can make.

Discuss It How do you know what shapes have been used to create each picture?

Practice Building Shapes

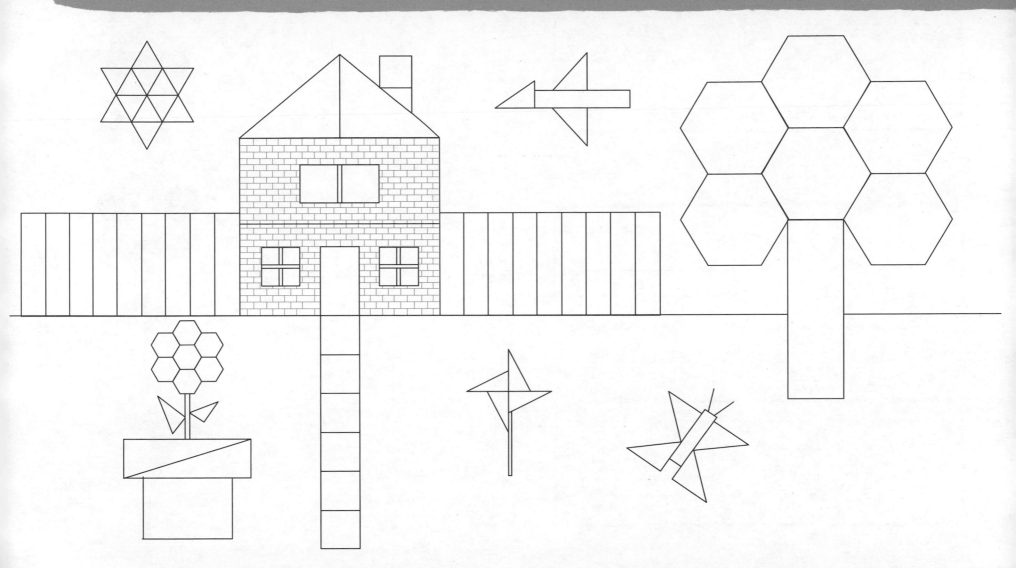

Have children use one color to color a rectangle that is made from triangles.
Then ask children to use a second color to color a square that is made from smaller squares and a third color to color a triangle that is made from smaller triangles. Have children color the rest of the picture.

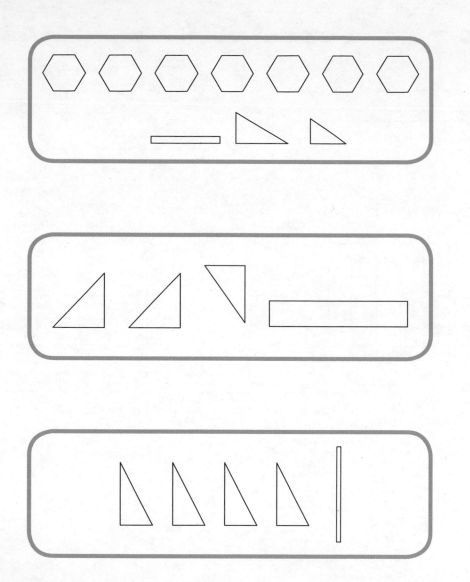

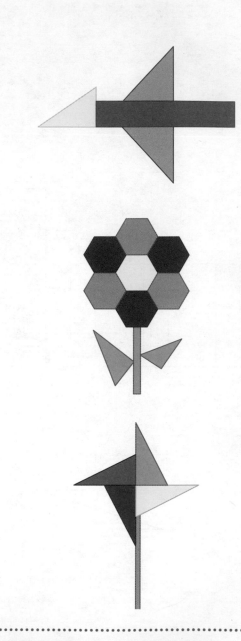

Ask children to identify small shapes within a larger shape. Have children look at the different shapes used to make each object. Then have children draw lines to match each group of smaller shapes to the object they can make.

Develop Building Shapes

Try It

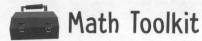 **Math Toolkit**

- toothpicks
- clay
- triangles and squares

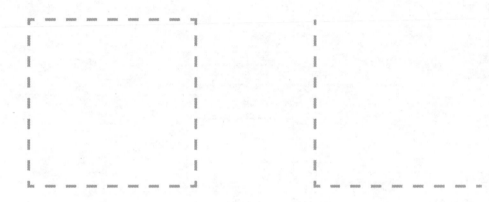

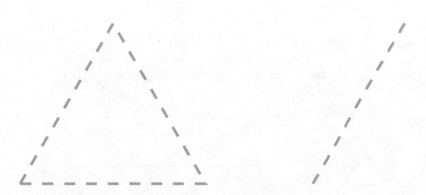

Have children build, trace, complete, and draw a square and a triangle. Give children toothpicks and small balls of clay to make a square and then a triangle. Have them join the toothpicks with the clay. Have children then trace, complete, and draw their own shapes.

 Discuss It How many toothpicks and balls of clay did you use to build each shape?

Lesson 15 Build Shapes **297**

Connect It

Ask children to use the colored shapes to make the outlined shape. Have children use cutouts of the shapes to try different arrangements. Have children draw lines or color to show how the shapes fit into the outlined shape.

 What other shapes could you use to make the outlined shapes?

Practice Building Shapes

Example

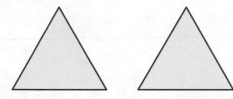 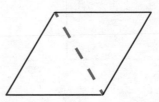

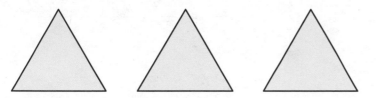 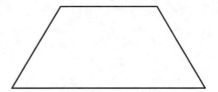

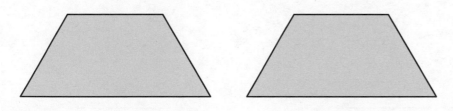 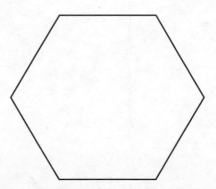

Ask children to use shapes like the colored shapes shown to make each outlined shape at the right. Have children use pattern blocks or copies of the colored shapes to try different arrangements for making the outlined shape at the right. Have children draw lines to show how the smaller shapes fit into the outlined shape.

©Curriculum Associates, LLC   Copying is not permitted.

Lesson 15 Build Shapes   **299**

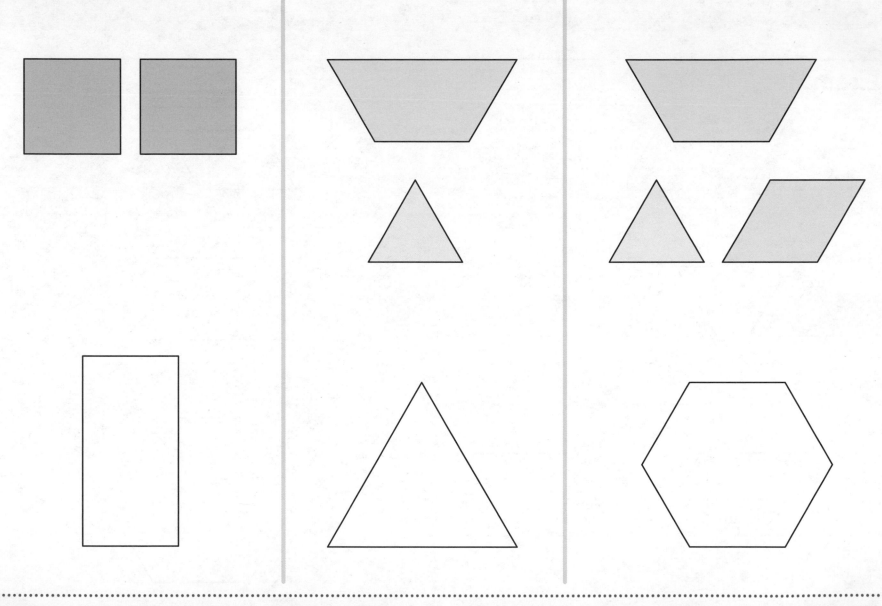

Ask children to use shapes like the colored shapes shown to make each outlined shape below. Have children use pattern blocks or copies of the colored shapes to try different arrangements for making the outlined shape below. Have children draw lines to show how the smaller shapes fit into the outlined shape.

300 **Lesson 15** Build Shapes

Refine Building Shapes

Apply It

 Math Toolkit
- blocks
- geometric solids

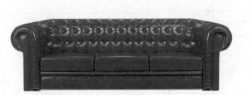

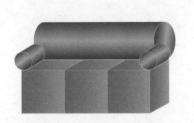

Have children use blocks to make new shapes. Give children a set of blocks. Ask them to put blocks together to build an object they can see or one they know, such as a tower, a bridge, etc. Have children look at the page and match the objects with the block shapes.

Discuss It How can you put blocks together to make new shapes? Can you make some of the objects on the page?

Lesson 15 Build Shapes **301**

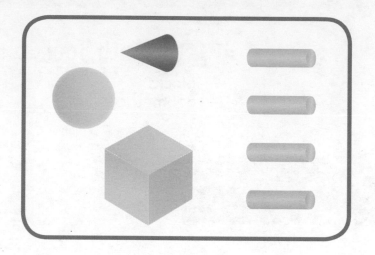

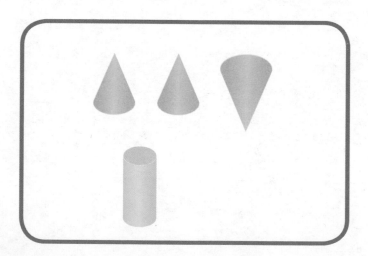

Have children find which model was made from the group of shapes in each box. Have children look at the different shapes. Then have them ring (circle) the object that matches the group of smaller shapes used to make that object.

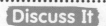 What shapes have been used to make the other objects? How do you know?

Practice Building Shapes

Example

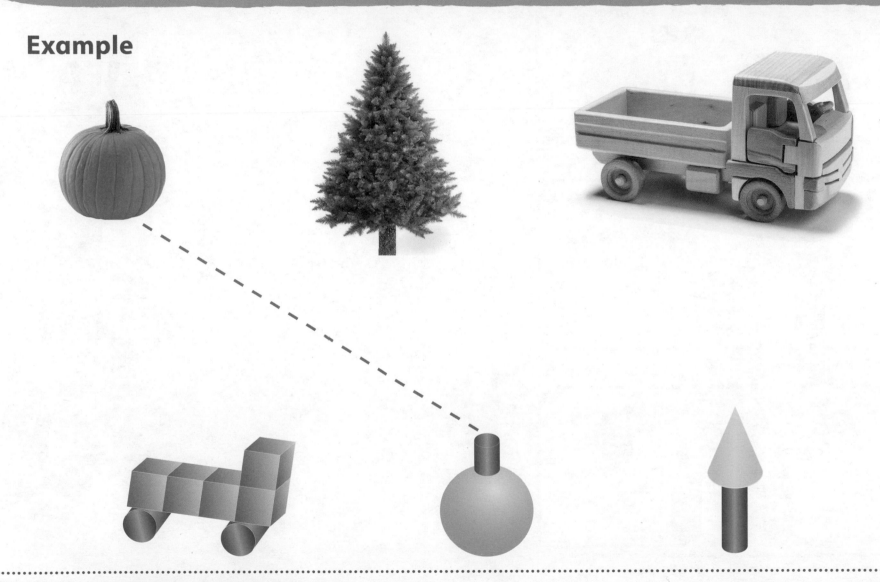

Have children match the pictures to the block shapes. Look at the pictures and shapes with children. Have children draw lines to match the objects with the block shapes.

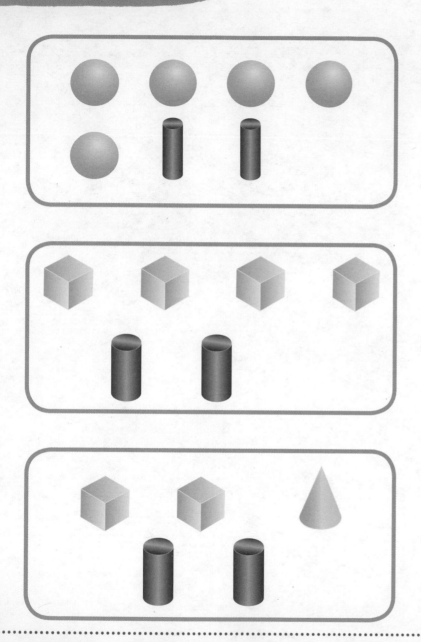

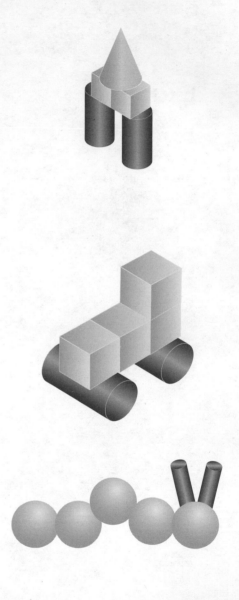

Ask children to match the groups of shapes to the objects that can be built with them. Have children find the objects made from the solid shapes.

Then have them draw lines to match each group of smaller shapes to the object they can make.

Refine Building Shapes

Apply It

Math Toolkit
- toothpicks
- clay

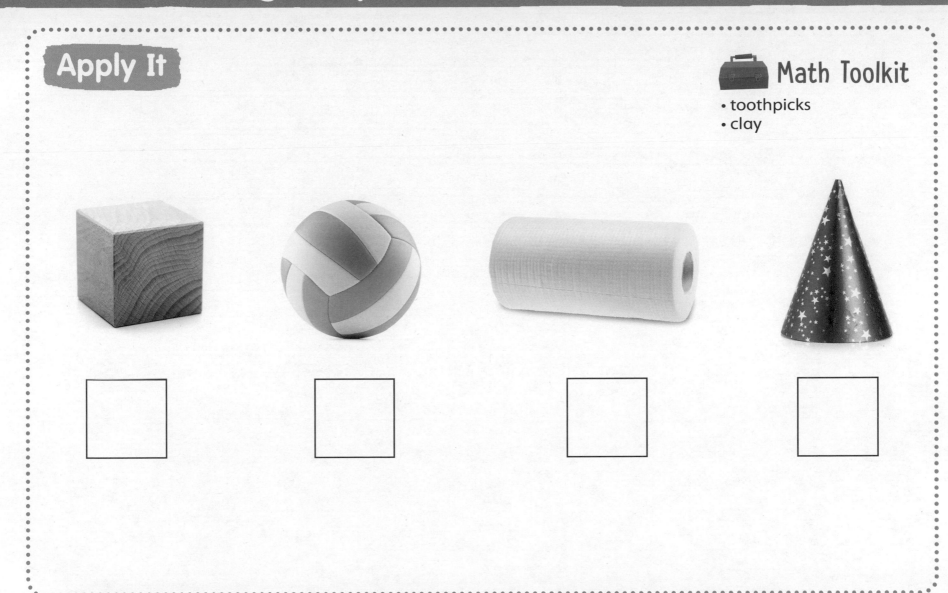

Have children make solid shapes. Have children use toothpicks and clay to model the shape of the block. Have them describe the shape they made. Then have children use just clay to model the other shapes and put a check mark by each one when completed.

Discuss It How can you use clay to make solid shapes? Describe each of the shapes you made.

Have children combine shapes to make a picture. Have children use the guidelines to color triangles and squares to make a picture or pattern of their own design.

Discuss It Work with a partner. How are your pictures alike? How are your pictures different?

Show What You Learned

Have children draw to show what they learned about shapes. Prompt children to reflect on their learning by posing questions such as: *What was the hardest math you learned? Why? What would you like to know more about? What could you use more practice with?*

For the top problem, have children ring (circle) the ball that is below a chair and mark an X on the ball that is beside a chair. For the bottom problem, have children ring (circle) all the cubes.

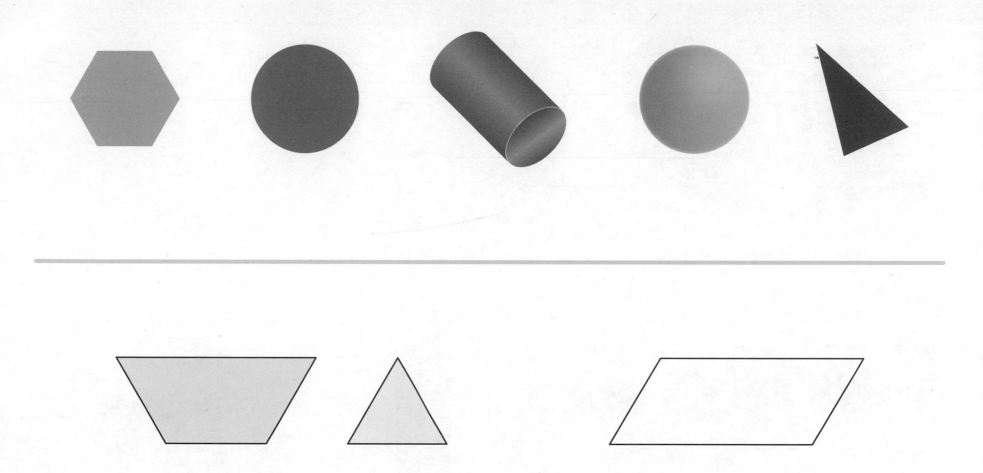

For the top problem, have children ring (circle) all the flat shapes and mark an X on all the solid shapes. For the bottom problem, have children draw lines on the large shape to show how the smaller shapes can be arranged to make the large shape.

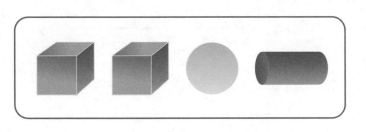

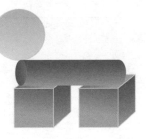

For the top problem, have children ring (circle) the shapes with curves.
For the bottom problem, have children ring (circle) the object that matches
the group of smaller shapes used to make that object.

Aa

above • sobre

add • sumar

2   +   1   =   3

addend • sumando

2   +   3   =   5

addends

Bb

behind • detrás de

below • debajo de

beside • junto a

Cc

circle • círculo

compare height • comparar la altura

compare length • comparar la longitud

compare numbers • comparar números

3

5

compare weight • comparar el peso

cone • cono

corner • esquina

count • contar

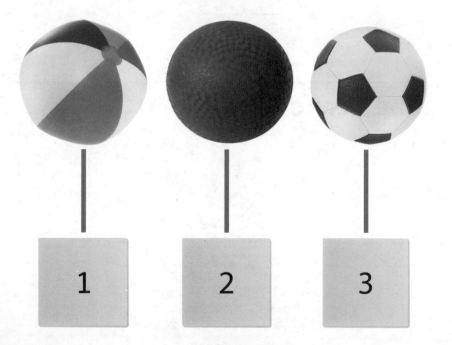

| 1 | 2 | 3 |

count on • contar hacia delante

| 10 | 11 | 12 | 13 |

cube • cubo

cylinder • cilindro

Dd

digit • dígito

25

Ee

edge • arista

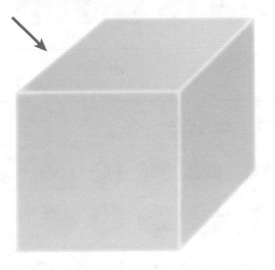

eight • ocho

8

eighteen • dieciocho

18

eleven • once

11

equal • igual

3

3

equal sign (=) • signo de igual (=)

$$2 \quad + \quad 3 \quad = \quad 5$$

↑

equation • ecuación

$$6 \quad - \quad 2 \quad = \quad 4$$

Ff

face • cara

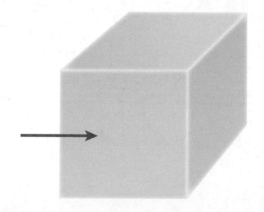

fewer, fewer than • menos, menos que

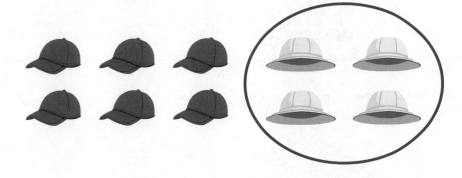

fifteen • quince

15

five • cinco

5

four • cuatro

4

fourteen • catorce

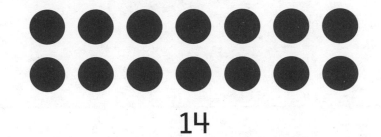

14

Gg

greater, greater than • mayor, mayor que

3

5

Hh

heavier • más pesado

heavy • pesado

height • altura

hexagon • hexágono

Ii

in front of • delante de

Ll

length • longitud

less, less than • menos, menos que

③

5

light • liviano

lighter • más liviano

long • largo

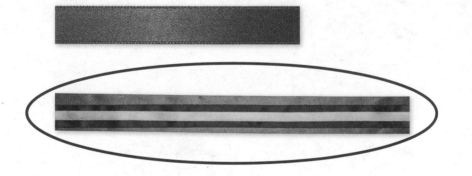

longer • más largo

Mm

minus sign (−) • signo menos (−)

$$5 \quad - \quad 3 \quad = \quad 2$$

more, more than • más, más que

Nn

next to • al lado de

nine • nueve

9

nineteen • diecinueve

19

number • número

5

number bond • enlace numérico

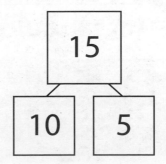

Oo

one • uno

1

Pp

plus sign (+) • signo más (+)

2 + 3 = 5

Rr

rectangle • rectángulo

Ss

seven • siete

7

seventeen • diecisiete

17

short • bajo

shorter • más corto

---

side • lado

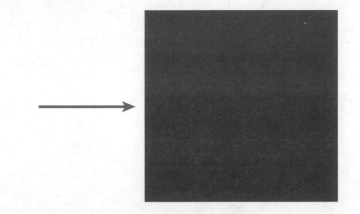

---

six • seis

6

sixteen • dieciséis

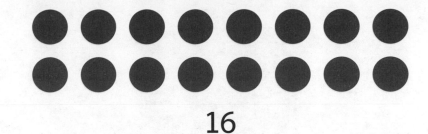

16

---

sort • clasificar

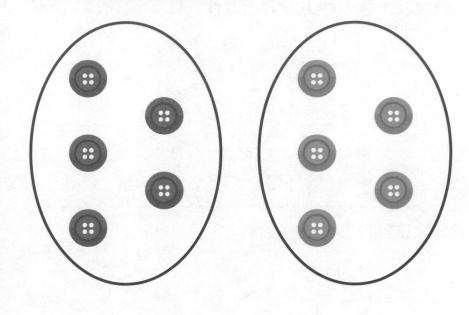

sphere • esfera

---

square • cuadrado

---

subtract • restar

$$3 - 1 = 2$$

tall • alto

---

taller • más alto

teen numbers • números del 11 al 19

| 11 | 12 | 13 | 14 | 15 | 16 | 17 | 18 | 19 |

ten • diez

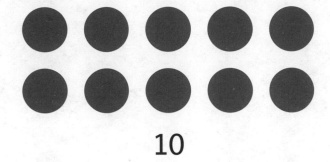

10

thirteen • trece

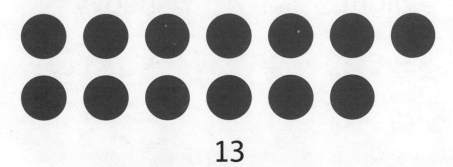

13

three • tres

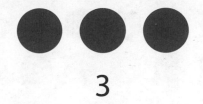

3

total • total

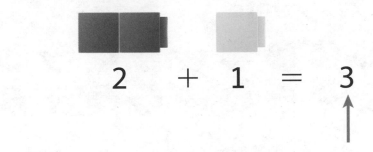

2 + 1 = 3

triangle • triángulo

twelve • doce

12

twenty • veinte

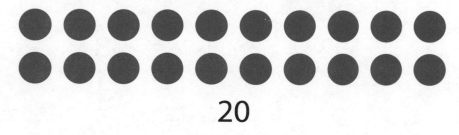

20

two • dos

2

Ww

weight • peso

light   heavy

Zz

zero • cero

0 fish

Acknowledgments

Common Core State Standards © 2010. National Governors Association Center for Best Practices and Council of Chief State School Officers. All rights reserved.

Photography Credits

United States coin images (unless otherwise indicated) from the United States Mint

Images used under license from **Shutterstock.com**.

Front Cover Danilaleo, Kamira, kool99, Robert Lessman; **vi** Ekaterina Abrosimova, Markus Mainka; **3** Yellow Cat, Dmitrij Skorobogatov, Triling Studio Ltd; **4** Jiang Hongyan, Elbud, LittleMiss; **5** Tom Gowanlock; **6** nuttakit; **8** SnapCraft; **20** Hong Vo, Anton Starikov, Mega Pixel; **39** Kostiantyn Fastov, smilewithjul; **40** Jiang Hongyan, Andrew Burgess, Roberaten; **45** Jajaladdawan; **50** Djmilic, r.classen, Enchanted_fairy; **51** Starikov, Mega Pixel, Insago; **52** Ruth Black; **55** BorisShevchuk; **59** HeinzTeh; **60** OnlyZoia; **65** Two over Two Studio; **72** KimHD, Preto Perola, Dmitrij Skorobogatov, FocusStocker, Iasha; **79** Photosync, Ispace, marssanya; **80** Wealthylady, showcake; **84** VanReeel; **85** Mardoz; **89** Kaspri; **99** Antpkr; **100** FocusStocker; **102** cynoclub, r.classen; **104** DenisNata; **105** Cynoclub, Prostock-studio, Picsfive; **106** artnLera, Vitaly Korovin, Smit, mhatzapa; **111** Zffoto; **115** artnLera, Africa Studio; **119** Smit; **123** mhatzapa, Eric Isselee, liskus; **124** r.classen; **125** mhatzapa, Anita Patterson Peppers, Butterfly Hunter, liskus; **126** Food Travel Stockforlife, Vitaly Zorkin, showcake; **127** Picsfive; **136–138** ntstudio; **141** artnLera, Ermolaev Alexander; **142** Anton Starikov, Africa Studio; **147** Smereka; **151** Monkeyoum; **159** Andrew Burgess **161** Tatyana Vyc; **162** AzriSuratmin; **166** stockcreations; **171** Passakorn Umpornmaha, Glass and Nature, Lightspring, Picsfive, Andrei Kuzmik, Mega Pixel, nehls16321, nelik, Africa Studio, Vorobyeva, oksana2010, Petr Malyshev, Chones; **172** cynoclub, Tatyana Vyc, Tim UR, Chones, bergamont, Lisa A. Svara, Eric Isselee, nelik, duangnapa_b; **173** Shebeko, bergamont, ntstudio, Nataliia K, kittipong kongwatmai, Tsveta Nesheva, Serg64, irin-k, Dora Zett, Natalia K, Eric Isselee, Lisa A. Svara; **174** HomeArt, pukach, Yellow Cat, Nata_Smilyk art, vipman's, Tim UR, bergamont, LZ Image, Danny Smythe, Jjustas Tim UR; **176** William Milner, BalancePhoto, Maksim Toome, Danny Smythe, EHStockphoto, Marisa Lia, Mtsaride, magicoven, Eric Isselee, Dimitris Leonidas, Anest; **177** Denis Pepin, Mega Pixel, aperturesound, Zhukovskaya Elena, Iasha, Vorotylin Roman, Andrei Kuzmik, Chones; **178** nattanan726, Eric Isselee, Glass and Nature, Butterfly Hunter, Passakorn Umpornmaha, Potapov Alexander, photomaster; **180** Preto Perola; **181** Yanugkelid; **182** Piyaset, Preto Perola, Africa Studio; **187** Chloe7992, **190** Charles Shapiro, Pixfiction, Chones, Utekhina Anna; **221** Eric Isselee; **224** oksana2010, DenisNata, Timothy Geiss; **228** Mega Pixel, Akugasahagy, Evannovostro, urfin, valdis torms, Chones, photogal, Denis Kovin, mhatzapa; **233** SomchaiP; **241** Mega Pixel, Tim UR, jeabsam, gmstockstudio, urfin, Chones, Resul Muslu, Brooke Becker, Mariyana M; **247** Handies Peak, SAPhotog, Ruslan Ivantsov, erashov, Sheila Fitzgerald, Fotoksa, Mega Pixel, Kletr, artnLera; **248** Abramova Elena, Sheila Fitzgerald; **253** Michelle Marsan; **254** VectorPic; **257** Brooke Becker, Matt Benoit, Sara van Netten, ColinCramm; **258** Mariyana M, Handies Peak, Kaspri, garyfox45114, Tim UR, Africa Studio, SAPhotog, Chones, jeabsam, baitong333, Mega Pixel; **259** de2marco, Vilaiporn Chatchawal, Michael Kraus, Mega Pixel, Maksym Bondarchuk, Sara van Netten, AzriSuratmin; **260** CHAIYARAT, Keith Bell, Diana Rich, magicoven, Fotoksa, Viktor1, valdis torms, Catinsyrup; **261** urfin; **262** Sergii Tverdokhlibov, urfin, Bennian, Eric Isselee, CharacterFamily Mega Pixel;

263 Bennian, Chones, Bluebloodbkk, nevodka, Maks Narodenko, Eric Isselee, Lisa A. Svara; **264** CharacterFamily, Dontree, J.Gatherum, Sergii Tverdokhlibov, Eric Isselee, nelik, Lightspring, Nejron Photo, Gts, oksana2010, Picsfive; **265** Bejim; **267** FocusStocker, Anton Starikov, Byggarn.se, Hank Shiffman, Mhatzapa; **268** Gts, Digipear, Lennon Schneider, mhatzapa; **273** Somporn Wongvichienkul; **281** Gts, Bennian, Maks Narodenko, Mariyana M, CharacterFamily; **287** Nenov Brothers Images, Marssanya; **288** Nonnakrit, BWFolsom; **293** Vovan; **301** Vadym Andrushchenko; **303** Beloborod; **305** Laborant, Monticello, Ugorenkov Aleksandr, pryzmat; **307** redstone; **308** Chones, Bejim; **313** Seregam, MrBright, Bergamont; **314** Hong Vo, Africa Studio; **320** Bergamont; **322** Utekhina Anna; **329** Le Do; **330** Nik Merkulov, AlenKadr, Irina Rogova; **335** dcwcreations; **340** Eric Isselee, Little Perfect Stoc, Olhastock, Lightspring, Butterfly Hunter, takoburito, DenisNata; **341** FocusStocker, n7atal7i, Valentina Razumova, stockphoto-graf; **342** Aleksey Stemme, Picsfive, bergamont, Maks Narodenko, SunshineVector; **343** bergamont, Butterfly Hunter, Lightspring, Picsfive; **344** bergamont, Lightspring, Butterfly Hunter, stockphoto-graf; **345** Aleksey Stemme, Yellow Cat, N7atal7i; **346** Tatyana Vyc, Topseller, bergamont, Dan Thornberg, FocusStocker; **349** Nejron Photo, Angeliki Vel; **350** MyImages – Micha, Lifestudio, Zeligen, Marssanya, Natasha Pankina; **356**, **358** Preto Perola; **365** Aleksey Troshin, Africa Studio, ExpressVectors; **366** Carolyn Franks, Palform, Blue67design, Pukach, Tatiana Popova; **371** Ntstudio; **380** Madlen, Aleksandr Bagri, Aleksey Troshin; **381** Preto Perola, Madlen, Aleksandr Bagri; **382** Danilaleo, Aleksey Troshin, Hurst Photo; **385** Ivonne Wierink, liskus; **386** Fotolotos, artnLera; **390** Mile Atanasov, artnLera; **399** xpixel, Eric Isselee; **402** Ivonne Wierink; **405** Africa Studio, Olllikeballoon; **406** Thomas Soellner, April Turner; **407** Natasha Pankina; **410** Africa Studio; **411** TigerStock's; **418** Oleksandr Lytvynenko, otsphoto, Rich Carey, StudioSmart, Tsekhmister, JIANG HONGYAN; **420** Tsekhmister, JIANG HONGYAN; **421** suns07butterfly, Kosarev Alexander, Kucher Serhii, Preto Perola; **424** Eric Isselee, absolutimages; **425** Dionisvera; **426** Nik Merkulov, Africa Studio; **431** acceptphoto; **444** Pixfiction; **445** Thitisan, liskus, Redchocolate; **446** photka, Drakuliren, primiaou; **451** Quang Vu; **457** Nitr, Africa Studio, Anna Kucherova, Eric Isselee, mexrix; **458** Miiisha, loskutnikov, Maslov Dmitr, Aksenova Natalya, Kapustin Igor, Tetiana Rostopira; **459** Picsfive; **460–461** Prostock-studio, photka, Picsfive; **462** Picsfive; **463** Eric Isselee; **465** nevodka, Petr Malyshev, Nik Merkulov, Apr-70, smilewithjul; **466** Nik Merkulov, Kelvin Wong, smilewithjul, Lalahouse; **471** Boumen Japet; **477** Benjawan phurit, Happymay; **478** Chones; **485** Fekete Tibor, Eric Isselee, liskus, Jody Ann; **486** Petr Malyshev, Apr-70, liskus; **490** Kaiskynet Studio, Volkova Anna; **491** suwatsilp sooksang; **500**; **505** Ivonne Wierink, liskus; **506** Picsfive, enchanted_fairy; **512** Prostock-studio, Mega Pixel, IB Photography; **527** xpixel, Gumenyuk Dmitriy, Wonderful Future World; **528** Marina Yesina, Bachkova Natalia, Nadisja, Zeligen; **530** Exopixel; **533** Stanislaw Mikulski; **539** Yellow Cat, Vorobyeva; **540** ecco, Bennian; **546** Africa Studio; **547** Mega Pixel, IB Photography; **548** mayakova, Graphic.mooi,

Illustration Credits

All Illustrations by **Tim Chi Ly**

olllikeballoon, Erica Truex; **567** EtiAmmos, Madlen; **568** Koosen, BravissimoS, liskus, marssanya; **569** chuchiko17; **570** klenger; **572** Revers; **573** David Franklin; **578** Studio DMM Photography, Design and Art; Designs & Art, EtiAmmos, Madlen; **579** EtiAmmos, Madlen, Goldnetz; **580** Pukach, Watchara Phochareung, Studio DMM Photography Design and Art; **587** Photosync, Lina_Lisichka, Balabolka; **588** Pakpoom Phummee, BLKstudio, gan chaonan, Ken StockPhoto, sarayuth3390; **589** Swill Klitch; **593–594** NumbSt; **607** Ravi; **608** Marques; **611** acceptphoto; **613** FabrikaSimf, Pixel B, Vorobyeva; **614** Yellow Cat, MichaelJayBerlin, Utekhina Anna, LightField Studios, Olizabet; **615** Evikka, Lucy Liu; **616** photastic; **618** Andrey Lobachev; **619** Andrey Myagkov; **622** Lineicons freebird; **623** andregric, Sergey Ash; **625** photastic, NARUDON ATSAWALARPSAKUN, sergign, Siyapath, cynoclub; **626** Africa Studio, SergiyN, urfin, Dora Zett; **628** nopporn0510, Zerbor, robotrecorder, Jiri Vaclavek; **629** QMTstudio, Richard Peterson, timquo, ESOlex; **630** ingret, Eric Isselee, Brooke Becker, Laboko; **632** Vorobyeva, gdvcom; **633** HeinzTeh, niwat chaiyawoot, Photo Melon, Potapov Alexander, Lano4ka, Mhatzapa; **634** MustafaNC, yauhenka, KK Tan, Little birdie, Zeligen, kostolom3000; **635** Chinnapong; **636** BlueRingMedia, Yellow Cat, Sondre Lysne; **638** pticelov, AVS-Images, Boltenkoff, 7th Son Studio; **639** Icosha; **645** Iakov Filimonov, topseller, Gts, pukach, kzww, Maks Narodenko, stockphoto-graf, Picsfive, FocusStocker, Valentina Razumova, 7th Son Studio; **646** kzww, Danilaleo, Ratikova, gts, MustafaNC, Sondre Lysne, Yellow Cat, Yarkovoy, Albo003, Keith Homan, csivasz, sergign; **647** Ladislav Berecz; **649** Mtsaride, Tim UR, Dan Thornberg, pukach, Keith Homan, topseller, Albo003, Picsfive, niwat chaiyawoot, kzww; **650** bergamont, Infinity T29, Iakov Filimonov, 7th Son Studio, sergign, Yellow Cat, Valentina Razumova, Ratikova, csivasz, Sondre Lysne, Danny Smythe, Gts; **651** JpeglonitaPhotographer; **652** Keith Homan; **653** Dionisvera, HomeArt; **654** Richard Peterson, cynoclub, ESB Professional; **655** Yellow Cat, Valentina Razumova, loskutnikov; **656** MustafaNC, cynoclub, urfin; **A1** urfin, Eric Isselee, Mega Pixel; **A2** urfin, Utekhina Anna, nopporn0510, Zerbor; **A3** MustafaNC, HomeArt; **A4**; **A8**; **A8** MustafaNC, HomeArt, Picsfive, nopporn0510; **A9** Eric Isselee, Mega Pixel, gdvcom, Picsfive, HomeArt; **A10** MustafaNC, HomeArt, Pixel B, FabrikaSimf; **A11** Utekhina Anna; **A12** Vorobyeva; **A13** photastic; **A14** nopporn0510, Zerbor; **A16** Picsfive, HomeArt; **A17** r. Classen

Student Handbook, appearing in Student Bookshelf and Teacher Guide only:
HBi ArtMari, Pixfiction, Rawpixel.com; **HB1** Pixfiction, Africa Studio, ArtMari; **HB2** iadams, ArtMari; **HB3** Palabra, ArtMari; **HB4** Tero Vesalainen, ArtMari; **HB5** Harvepino, ArtMari; **HB6–HB7** ArtMari **HB8** Chiyacat, ArtMari; **HB9** Kyselova Inna, Markus Mainka, ArtMari; **HB10** ArtMari